# Project Stakeholder Engagement



*Project Stakeholder Engagement* provides concepts and frameworks that can help the reader gain insights into a project's stakeholders, and how to engage them. It also gives suggestions for how to identify and understand stakeholders, and how to create an engagement plan with communication and other activities.

Readers will gain essential skills to drive project success by learning to systematically analyse stakeholders and develop targeted engagement strategies. The book delivers these benefits through research-based frameworks illustrated with real-world examples, mini-cases highlighting key concepts, and comprehensive case studies bridging theory and practice. Written primarily for undergraduate and postgraduate students in project management and business administration, this book is equally valuable for practising project managers, consultants, and executives seeking to enhance their stakeholder engagement skills. It's particularly relevant for courses in project management, project stakeholder engagement, and value creation.

Supporting materials include PowerPoint slides summarizing key frameworks, and an instructor's manual with teaching notes for case studies, facilitating effective classroom discussion and application of the book's principles.

**Pernille Eskerod** is professor of management and organizational behaviour at Webster Vienna Private University, Austria. She holds a Ph.D. in business administration and has a long academic career within project management, focusing on project stakeholder engagement. Pernille also teaches and supervises at the WU Executive Academy in Vienna. She has an extensive academic publication record, establishing herself as a leading authority in the field.

**Anna Lund Jepsen** is associate professor of economics and business administration at the University of Southern Denmark, Denmark. She holds a Ph.D. in economics and business administration. Anna's research focuses on project management, with particular emphasis on stakeholder engagement and project portfolio management. Her teaching experience includes numerous project management courses, working with both full-time students and professional master's students.

# Contents

# Figures

# Tables

# Boxes

# Mini-cases

# Preface

This book provides you with concepts and frameworks that can be used to structure your understanding of the project's stakeholders and help you work with them. A good understanding of theory will support you in achieving good results.

The book also provides suggestions on what you can do in practice, e.g. how to identify the project's stakeholders and their requirements, wishes and concerns, and how to create a communication plan that considers the characteristics of each stakeholder.

The book is filled with examples from everyday life, e.g. from construction projects that you see in the streets. Our idea is that these examples will inspire you to reflect on projects and stakeholders in your daily life. You can see projects and stakeholders everywhere, and you are a stakeholder yourself. Use the opportunities around you to sharpen your insight and understanding. It pays off.

To facilitate the understanding of the theoretical concepts, the book contains a mini-case at the end of each chapter, as well as comprehensive cases at the end of the book, which allow for discussion that draws on several chapters.

The book is an adapted version of our book in Danish on the same topic, *Projektets interessenter – analyse og samspil* [The project's stakeholders – analysis and engagement] (Djøf Forlag, 2025).

We thank Routledge for the opportunity to publish this book and the helpful editors and other staff for their kind advice and swift feedback along the way.

# 1 Stakeholder engagement

## A key to good project management

Projects are established to create value through positive changes. An example is a project aimed at creating better working conditions through a new office setup. Such a project needs financing from management, knowledge and time from employees, and new office equipment from a supplier. Management, employees, and the supplier can thus influence the project by providing these contributions to the project. However, the project also influences its environment, e.g. the employees, as it results in a new physical working environment. The project also influences the supplier through payment for the equipment. The employees, management, and the supplier are examples of ***project stakeholders***, who

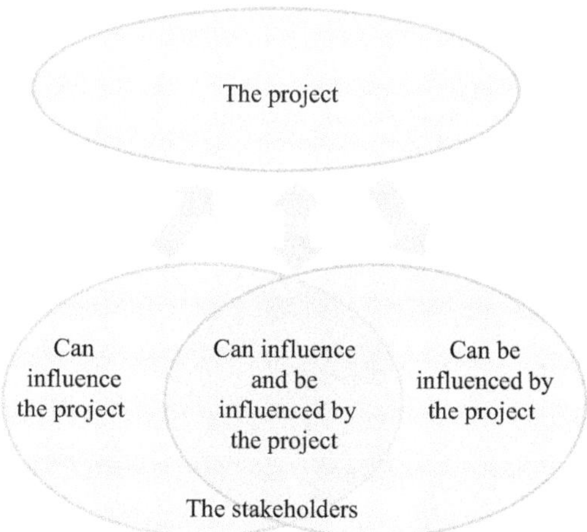


*Figure 1.1* The project and stakeholder influences

DOI: 10.4324/9781003712695-1

are *individuals and entities that can influence or be influenced by the project* (Eskerod & Jepsen, 2016). See Figure 1.1.

There are many different types of project stakeholders. Closest to the project, we see individuals or entities within the organization that established the project (*the base organization*). Examples of such stakeholders include decision-makers and departments with staff or expertise that the project needs. We also find important stakeholders in the immediate environment of the base organization such as customers, suppliers, and unions. Finally, in the non-immediate environment, we also find individuals and entities who can influence or be influenced by the project, such as public authorities or neighbours and others in the project's local community. See Figure 1.2 for an illustration of some typical project stakeholders.

To be successful, a project needs stakeholders to *contribute* to the project. They can do so either by providing resources or other forms of support to the project (*influence positively*), or by refraining to act in ways that will harm the project (*influence negatively*).

Maybe a stakeholder is thrilled to contribute and sees a lot of benefits from doing that. However, the opposite may also be true if the stakeholder is against the project and would prefer to spend his or her efforts and resources on something else. Whether the stakeholder can or will contribute to the project as needed is uncertain. A core task for the project manager is to actively work with the stakeholders to minimize this uncertainty. The project manager should do so by

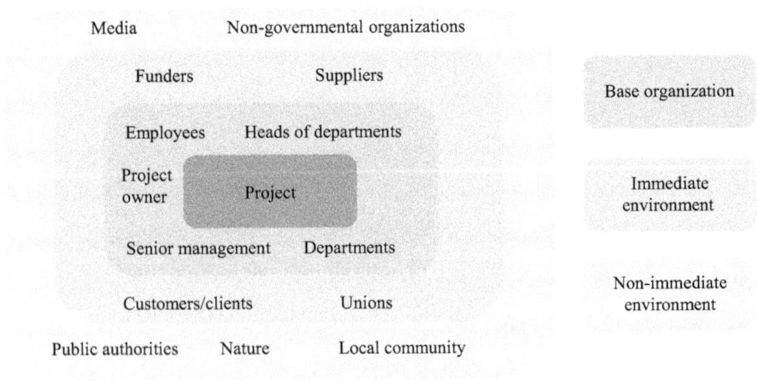


*Figure 1.2* Typical project stakeholders

setting up actions that will support stakeholder contribution based on an understanding of the stakeholder's expectations of the potential value from contributing to the project. This work is what *project stakeholder engagement* is about. We define project stakeholder engagement as *activities with and towards stakeholders aimed at ensuring that the project creates the intended value.*

In this book, we speak to you as the project manager, or another person working on the project, e.g. a project team member. These are who we mean when we write "you" in the book.

Box 1.1 provides an overview of foundational elements in project stakeholder engagement.

**Box 1.1 The foundation of project stakeholder engagement**

- Stakeholders are individuals and entities that can influence or be influenced by the project
- Stakeholders can influence and be influenced by the project positively, negatively, or both
- The project needs contributions from stakeholders
- Whether a stakeholder can and will contribute is an uncertainty in the project
- Through stakeholder engagement, the project manager can encourage stakeholder contribution
- Project stakeholder engagement refers to activities with and towards stakeholders aimed at ensuring that the project creates the intended value

## Project stakeholder engagement in brief

*Project stakeholder engagement* is about being proactive and prepared for what may happen. Being proactive means that you reflect on the project's needs and options and learn about the stakeholders and their perspective on contributing to the project. For some stakeholders, it is easy to see the value from contributing. This is, for example, the case for suppliers who obtain financial value from delivering project materials. Other stakeholders may find it more difficult to see the value in contributing. What does a user gain from testing a new product? Why should a department head send their best, most highly sought-after employee to a new project? Why should a concerned neighbour refrain from protesting a new subway? You can only answer these questions if you understand the stakeholders' perspectives on the project and on contributing to the project.

A stakeholder analysis can help you get the knowledge that you need to understand the stakeholders. It comprises stakeholder identification and assessment of the likelihood that each stakeholder will contribute, and thus the need for working on their engagement. Knowledge about stakeholders can be gathered in a *stakeholder register*, which can help you prioritize your efforts towards the stakeholders. Such a prioritization can help you spend your limited resources for project management, including engaging with the stakeholders, on the stakeholders who need the most attention at a given time during the project.

The information in the stakeholder register provides a good basis for assessing how you can work with each stakeholder to ensure their contribution. In general terms, there are two ways to go if a stakeholder is reluctant to contribute. You can adjust the project or you can work with the stakeholder's attitude towards contributing. In many cases, engaging stakeholders involves some of both. This book focuses on the possible actions that you, as a project manager, can take to engage the stakeholders, and only little on accommodating the stakeholders by adjusting the project. However, be aware that this option is often present.

Based on your knowledge about the stakeholders, you can create a well-thought-out *engagement plan* for your stakeholder engagement. An engagement plan can prevent you from getting carried away by a loud stakeholder in a heated moment. Perhaps this stakeholder is not the most important one to spend time on.

If you work purposefully with stakeholder engagement and set aside time to conduct stakeholder analyses and get to know your stakeholders, you can: (1) be ready to act at a time when you still have room to manoeuvre, (2) make well-thought-out decisions about the efficient use of the project's resources, and (3) throughout the project's life ensure its relevance through updated information about the stakeholders.

In addition to the planned stakeholder engagement, you will need to continually *improvise* your collaboration with the stakeholders. A thorough analysis of stakeholders can help you improvise appropriately. Knowing the stakeholders' perspectives on the project will help you act in an orderly and effective manner in unexpected situations that require intuition and flexibility.

## Structure of the book

The first chapters of the book set the framework for stakeholder engagement. They describe the development of the stakeholder concept and the basic elements of stakeholder engagement as a part of project management. The next part of the book is dedicated to the elements of stakeholder analysis: stakeholder identification, elements determining the stakeholder's likelihood to contribute, and prioritization of your effort towards the stakeholders. We also present methods for data collection for the stakeholder analysis. This part culminates in the stakeholder register. The following chapters focus on how to engage the stakeholders. We suggest an approach to stakeholder engagement and strategies for engagement with related ways to bring the strategies to life, including possible communication activities. This part culminates in the engagement plan. To prepare you for making good choices in your engagement with stakeholders, we conclude the book by discussing some of the ethical and other challenges that stakeholder engagement may present to you.

You can read the book from start to finish, or you can start by reading about the stakeholder analysis or about planning the stakeholder engagement and then address the historical development and the basic elements of stakeholder engagement.

In our research and teaching, we have become aware of a fact that has become our motto for the book, namely that *stakeholder engagement is complex but can be learned*. Stakeholder engagement is something you can practise. We wish you the best of luck with your stakeholder engagement, and we hope that the concepts, theories, and tools we present in the book contribute positively to your efforts.

**Mini-case 1 Frogs and toads as stakeholders**

The Fehmarnbelt infrastructure megaproject plans to construct a tunnel for car and train traffic between Germany and Denmark. Environmental impacts are assessed in an Environmental Impact Assessment (EIA) report, which was initiated in response to legislative requirements and the project's own desire to prioritize nature conservation. The EIA has cost €66 million, 1 percent of the project budget. It took four years to complete.

The EIA report showed, among other things, that the project would severely impact the living conditions for frogs and toads. Water holes would be destroyed, and many frogs and toads might be killed by activities at the construction site.

The project found and included a solution for the benefit of frogs and toads in the project plan and budget. An expert in the form of a freshwater biologist from a consulting company helped the project with this work. To ensure the survival of frogs and toads, a so-called amphibian fence was established, so that the frogs and toads could only jump out from, but not into, the construction site, and in addition, the frogs and toads were given 26 new water holes to romp in.

Sources: Femern bælt (2025), Femern VVM (2025), and Marfelt (2013)

*The case illustrates how a project can incorporate stakeholders who may be influenced by negative side effects. In many projects, a preliminary investigation is required by the authorities. The case shows that this can take several years and add to the costs of the project.*

*The case also illustrates that non-humans can be stakeholders. These stakeholders may be unable to look after their own interests. In this case, an expert in the form of a freshwater biologist takes care of the interests of frogs and toads.*

## References

Eskerod, P., & Jepsen, A. L. (2016). *Project stakeholder management.* Routledge.

Femern bælt (2025). *Vi bygger med naturen* [We build with nature]. https://femern.com/da/. Accessed 9 August 2025.

Femern VVM (2025). *Hvad er en VVM-redegørelse?* [What is an EIA report?]. https://vvmdokumentation.femern.dk/da. Accessed 9 August 2025.

Marfelt, B. (2013). *Femern afslutter danmarkshistoriens største VVM-undersøgelse* [Fehmarn completes the largest EIA study in Danish history]. Web article published 13 June. https://ing.dk/artikel/femern-afslutter-danmarkshistoriens-stoerste-vvm-undersoegelse.

# 2 The stakeholder concept

## Origin and development

If you are going to work with stakeholders, it is good to know what the stakeholder concept covers and its origin. Therefore, in this chapter we provide an outline of the development of the concept, and we describe the stakeholder concept in recent research.

### The stakeholder concept

The stakeholder concept originates from *having a stake in something*. This means that something is important to the person in question, because the person has an interest in it – the person has something at stake. We can see a project and a stakeholder as two parties who have a relationship from which both parties can gain or lose – they can be influenced positively or negatively. The parties both have a vested interest in getting the most out of the relationship. *The project* has the interest that those who can *positively influence the project* do so. For example, they can allocate staff, expertise, and financial and other resources to the project. The project also has the interest that those who can *negatively influence the project* refrain from doing so. For example, they can refrain from withholding resources or protesting the project. Finally, those who *may be influenced* by the project have an interest in being influenced in a way that is positive, or at least neutral. For example, they may want to experience as few inconveniences as possible from an office reshuffle, a construction project, or a nearby rock concert.

DOI: 10.4324/9781003712695-2

## Origin of the concept

In 1984, the book *Strategic management: A stakeholder approach* was published in the USA. In the book, the author, a 32-year-old American professor, R. Edward Freeman, who conducted research on strategic management and business ethics, encouraged business leaders to focus on stakeholders in their strategic management instead of solely on the group of owners (*stockholders*).

Freeman (1984) defined stakeholders as "any group or individual who can affect or is affected by the achievement of the organization's objectives" (p. 25). Freeman's argument was that the existing theories on strategic management were unfit for the company environment of the 1980s because the world had increased in complexity. Many groups besides the owners could now influence (affect) the company and be influenced by it for good or for bad. Freeman (1984) mentioned several groups of stakeholders, emphasizing that these were just *examples*: owners, customers, employees, suppliers, authorities, competitors, consumer representatives, local community representatives, environmental activists, media, and special interest groups.

Freeman (1984) wrote that a way to analyse stakeholders within classical management thinking would be to depict them in a grid with the two dimensions: stake (or interest) and power. He pointed out three types of interest (stake): equity (owners), economic (market), and influencers (interest groups). He also pointed to three types of power: formal, economic, and political. The analysis would often be done by assigning each stakeholder to one combination of stake and power. However, Freeman pointed out that this is a simplification, as stakeholders often belong to more than one combination, e.g. as stockholders (equity power) and customers (economic power) of the same company. Including this in the analysis would make it messy, which is why Freeman suggested that "we must find innovative ways of understanding both the power and stakes of a variety of influential and interconnecting stakeholder groups" (Freeman, 1984, p. 63). Freeman (1984) further suggested that management must include all the company's stakeholders in its decisions to manage a company effectively and coined this a *stakeholder approach*.

Freeman was not the first to introduce the stakeholder concept. In his book, he points to others who have dealt with aspects of a stakeholder approach before him. For example, a Swedish professor, Eric

Rhenman, published a book in Swedish as early as 1964, *Företagsdemokrati och företagsorganisation*. The book was translated into English with the title *Industrial democracy and industrial management*, in 1968. The Swedish version of the book used the Swedish term for stakeholder, *intressent*, while the translated book used the term *stakeholder*. Rhenman introduced stakeholders to his readers and illustrated the stakeholders as rose petals around the organization. This figure was later called *Rhenman's rose*. Rhenman's focus was on corporate democracy and not on stakeholders as such. This can be seen from the fact that, in 1973, he published the book *Managing the community hospital: Systems analysis of a Swedish hospital*, where he used the concept of the *organization's participants* together with his rose instead of the concept of stakeholders.

Another early proponent of a stakeholder approach was the American researcher Aubrey L. Mendelow. At a conference in 1981, and in a follow-up article in an academic journal, he suggested that, to survive in the long term, an organization must monitor the stakeholders in the organization's environment. How closely each stakeholder must be monitored depends on two dimensions: the power of the stakeholder and the dynamic of the stakeholder – that is, how quickly the stakeholder can be expected to change (Mendelow, 1981, 1983). The two dimensions form a matrix. Mendelow points to four forms of power: possession of resources (that the stakeholder is the only one who can provide a necessary resource); dictation of alternatives (that the stakeholder can determine the alternative actions); authority (the right to enforce obedience); and influence on others (Mendelow, 1983). The four forms of power are in line with the types of power that Freeman (1984) mentions.

According to Mendelow, dynamic stakeholders with high power must be monitored closely. Dynamic stakeholders with low power must be monitored at regular intervals. Non-dynamic stakeholders with high power can be monitored as needed. It is not necessary to monitor non-dynamic stakeholders with low power. In an adapted version of Mendelow's matrix, the dynamic characteristic was replaced by interest (Johnson & Scholes, 1993). In this matrix, stakeholders with high power and high interest are labelled *key players*. They must be monitored closely. Stakeholders with low power and high interest should be kept informed and are sometimes labelled *keep informed* or *hostages*. Stakeholders with high power and low interest should be kept satisfied and are sometimes labelled *keep satisfied* or *grey eminences*. The organization should not spend resources on stakeholders with low power and low interest. This matrix's categorization of stakeholders is still widely used and referred to as the *power-interest* matrix or Mendelow's matrix.

Freeman's 1984 book was of enormous importance in making the stakeholder concept and the stakeholder approach known among both practitioners and researchers, and in taking them further in complexity and insights than earlier proponents. It is therefore fair to see Freeman as the founder of the stakeholder approach. The book is still read, and to this day Freeman remains one of the globally most active researchers in the field.

It is worth noting that stakeholder management, already according to Freeman's early work, is not about furthering the organization's objectives at the expense of the stakeholders' interest. According to Freeman, it is wrong to think that an ethical approach and a business approach to stakeholders are opposites. If you treat your stakeholders well, they will contribute better to the operation of the company, and this will lead to greater business success in the long run (Freeman, 1984).

Freeman and Rhenman both dealt with companies and not with projects. The American professor David I. Cleland, who is considered the founder of project management (Knutson, 2002), introduced the stakeholder concept in project management literature. This happened in the articles "A strategy for ongoing project evaluation" and "Project stakeholder management" in the *Project Management Journal* in 1985 and 1986, respectively. Before that, he had used the concept in a book from 1978 on strategic business management, *Strategic planning and policy*, written with his colleague William R. King. In the book, King and Cleland presented a method for analysing customers, claimants, and other stakeholders, and Cleland further developed the methods in the two articles. He pointed out that the project should identify the stakeholders and their strengths and weaknesses. This knowledge should be used to predict the stakeholders' behaviour, giving a foundation for decisions on how to work with the stakeholders.

## Creating and destroying value

Freeman et al. (2010) point out that a stakeholder approach "is about value creation and trade and how to manage a business effectively.

'Effective' can be seen as 'create as much value as possible'" (p. 9). Harrison and Wicks (2013) suggest looking at *value* as *the aggregated utility* (financial and non-financial). This is the additional value that the organization and the stakeholder get from their mutual engagement in the present activity. According to Harrison and Wicks (2013), value should be viewed very broadly. In a project context, this means that, for example, learning from collaboration with a stakeholder is also part of the project's value creation.

Unfortunately, an organization's *activities to create value can destroy value* for the stakeholders (Harrison & Wicks, 2021). This is also pointed out by Freeman et al. (2020). They state: "Every business has always created and sometimes destroyed multiple forms of value (e.g. financial, intellectual, social, emotional, spiritual, cultural, and ecological) for customers, suppliers, employees, communities, and financiers" (Freeman et al., 2020, p. 225). For example, production processes use resources that are taken from nature. This possible destruction of value means that organizations must assess the overall value of an activity, e.g. a project. The assessment of value created by an activity should include both the value to be generated by the activity and the value that the activity may destroy for the stakeholders (Harrison & Wicks, 2021). Such an assessment will be more complete than if only the value generated is assessed. It can also prepare the organization for possible negative reactions in the form of, for example, potential lawsuits, damaged reputation, lost sales, reduced motivation, or lost loyalty from stakeholders who stand to lose value (Harrison & Wicks, 2021).

To destroy as little value as possible, one must, according to Freeman (1995), assess how a proposed new activity influences *the least well-off stakeholder*, understood as the stakeholder who will be most negatively influenced by the activity. Based on this assessment, measures must be taken to ensure that after the activity this stakeholder will have at least the same value as if the activity were not initiated. Freeman (1995) also suggests considering the relationship with each stakeholder as a contractual relationship (even if it is not actually one) and applying a *principle of externalities* (i.e. side effects). The principle states that "if a contract between A and B imposes a cost on C, then C [should have] the option to become a party to the contract, and the terms renegotiated" (Freeman, 1995, p. 43).

In recent years, research in project management has worked to identify value destruction that is particularly harmful to stakeholders. Locatelli et al. (2022, 2024) point to possible corruption, sexism, modern slavery, money laundering, inefficient use of resources, and waste of existing assets.

Emphasizing that assessment of the project's value creation is about more than whether it fulfils its purpose is also reflected in the current literature on project success. Ika and Pinto (2022) point out that an important element in assessing project success is a shared perception of success among key stakeholders. Assessing a project's success from a shared perception of success entails that stakeholders become a resource instead of an uncertainty, because they can contribute to the project's value generation. In this book, we apply this view on success. We emphasize that assessing the project's success should be based on the value that the project creates for the stakeholders, overall, not just for the base organization. We also emphasize that it is the stakeholders who assess whether the project is a success from their perspective, and that this is a subjective assessment.

## Sustainable project management

In 1987, the World Commission on Environment and Development (WCED) of the United Nations published a report, Our Common Future. The report is referred to as "the Brundtland Report" after the Commission's foreperson, Gro Harlem Brundtland. The report focused on sustainable development globally. It provided guidance on how the concept should be understood:

> Humanity has the ability to make development sustainable – to ensure that it meets the needs of the present without compromising the ability of future generations to meet their own needs ... Sustainable development requires meeting the basic needs of all and extending to all the opportunity to fulfil their aspirations for a better life.
>
> (WCED, 1987, pp. ES 7–8)

According to the report, sustainable development requires consideration of both present and future generations as stakeholders.

This view on stakeholders is echoed by Starik (1994), who suggests defining an organization's stakeholders as "any naturally occurring entity which affects or is affected by the organizational performance" (p. 90). This includes animals, plants, rocks, water, ecosystems, the sun-earth system, and the cosmos. It may seem overwhelming to have to think so broadly, but it has nonetheless become increasingly common to include nature and its beings as stakeholders.

A concept often associated with sustainability is the *triple bottom line*, which John Elkington coined in 1994 (Elkington, 2018), often depicted by the words profit, people, planet. The bottom line is a concept taken from accounting, where the profit (or the net value) can be found on the bottom line. With the concept of the triple bottom line, Elkington (2018) encourages organizations to not only focus on the financial bottom line; they must also consider how they affect the natural environment and persons inside and outside the organization, both positively and negatively.

Since projects are established to create positive change, they can contribute to sustainable development in society. The concept of sustainable project management is gaining ground in research and in business. One of the earliest definitions says:

> Sustainable Project Management is the planning, monitoring and controlling of project delivery and support processes, with consideration of the environmental, economical and social aspects of the life-cycle of the project's resources, processes, deliverables and effects, aimed at realising benefits for stakeholders, and performed in a transparent, fair and ethical way that includes proactive stakeholder participation.
>
> (Silvius & Schipper, 2014, p. 79)

The Silvius and Schipper definition focuses solely on the project process. However, Gareis et al. (2013) and Huemann and Silvius (2017) have pointed out that the project's outcome must also be considered when assessing whether a project is sustainable. The project process concerns *whether the project deliverables are generated in a sustainable way*, including whether the project's stakeholders, e.g. suppliers, behave sustainably, and whether the project behaves sustainably towards its stakeholders. The project outcome concerns the *use of the project's deliverables* – that is, whether the use of the project's deliverables helps support future generations, e.g. through the development of facilities that can produce renewable energy, such as wind turbines and solar cells. Gareis et al. (2013) and Huemann and Silvius (2017) use the terms *sustainability of the project* and *sustainability by the project* to distinguish between sustainability in the project process and sustainability as a result of the project.

Eskerod and Huemann (2024) suggest that the stakeholder aspect of sustainable project management should be guided by six principles, which are: inclusive stakeholder definition, value transparency, perceived fairness, future orientation, co-creation, and multiple engagement forms. Table 2.1 explains the content of each principle. The guidelines for stakeholder engagement that we recommend in the book are in line with the six principles.

## A wider sense of stakeholders

Organizations' activities can influence and be influenced by an unlimited number of individuals and entities, and they are not all equally important to take into consideration and spend resources on. But who should the organization include in its considerations? Freeman and Reed (1983) distinguish between a narrow and a wide sense of stakeholders. A narrow sense of stakeholders focuses on *the stakeholders the organization depends on* to ensure its continued survival. These can be, for example, employees, target customers, certain suppliers, certain authorities, and shareholders. A wide sense of stakeholders, on the other hand, focuses on "any identifiable group or individual who can affect the achievement of an organization's objectives or who is affected by the achievement of an organization's objectives" (Freeman & Reed, 1983, p. 91). Freeman and Reed (1983) encourage managers to work with the wide definition. This is in line with the ideas in Freeman's book from 1984.

Since Freeman (1984) there has been much debate among both researchers and practitioners about the concept of stakeholders, and there is still no generally accepted definition of who should be included as stakeholders (Kujala et al., 2022). However, there is a movement towards using a wide definition of who are to be included. For example, Gil (2023) argues that stakeholders who are not part of the market forces in connection with the operation of an organization (and a project, we would add) should be included, because this helps

*Table 2.1* Principles for stakeholder engagement in sustainable project management

| # | *Principle* | *Description* |
|---|---|---|
| 1 | Inclusive stakeholder definition | An inclusive stakeholder definition means that the project organization considers a wide range of current and future individuals and groups that are affected or feel affected by the project process and/or project deliverables/outcomes regardless of their power. |
| 2 | Value transparency | Value transparency means that the project organization is open about and communicates about value creation, value destruction, and value distribution due to the project process and the project outcomes. The project organization acknowledges that economic and non-economic values exist. They also consider that objective value and subjective value co-exist, and that subjective value is value attributed by the project stakeholders based on their individual utility function, the benefits they gain or lose. |
| 3 | Perceived fairness | Perceived fairness means that the project organization seeks to generate fairness on multiple dimensions: distributional (including compensation for value destruction), procedural, interpersonal, and informational. It is the perception of fairness by the project stakeholders that is relevant, i.e. fairness is a subjective concept. |
| 4 | Future orientation | Future orientation means that the project organization is focused on the consequences of the project process and/or project outcome timewise in the form of short-term, mid-term, and long-term consequences for the project stakeholders. |
| 5 | Co-creation | Co-creation means that the project organization strives to create solutions with the project stakeholders both when it comes to the project process and the project outcomes. The project organization applies the concept of co-creation and future making together with the project stakeholders, i.e. they aim to negotiate and manifest a common future. |
| 6 | Multiple engagement forms | Multiple engagement forms means that the project organization applies a broad range of methods to engage with the various project stakeholders, e.g. consult them, train them, and inform them, and use a wide range of media, including digital and in-person, to reach out to a wide audience and take away barriers of communicating and engagement. |

Source: Eskerod and Huemann (2024, p. 250)

the organization create greater overall value. Examples of ***non-market stakeholders*** are local communities and authorities (Gil, 2023) as well as family members of, for example, employees and owners (Signori & Fassin, 2023). Starik's (1994) very wide definition cited above, which includes ecosystems and the cosmos, may be seen in a more positive light in today's sustainability agenda.

It is not only the definition of stakeholders that has changed over time. The perception of stakeholders' influence on the project has also shifted. Recent literature on project stakeholders, e.g. Klein et al. (2019), points out that it is not in line with a pursuit of sustainability if stakeholders who can be very negatively influenced by a project only have a voice if they have power. In relation to a construction project, negatively influenced stakeholders without power could be, for example, neighbours of the construction site. In product development projects, it could be customers that depend on the product and have no alternatives. How projects can interact with such stakeholders has been a focus of project management research in recent years (e.g. Di Maddaloni & Davis, 2017; Klein et al., 2019; Vuorinen & Martinsuo, 2019; Di Maddaloni & Sabini, 2022; Chung et al., 2023). The general opinion seems to be that stakeholders that can be greatly influenced by the project should be enfranchised (included in the decision processes) (Klein et al., 2019), e.g. by having the opportunity to state their opinion.

## Stakeholder engagement in a contemporary perspective

Recent views on sustainability and whom organizations should include in their considerations impact how stakeholder engagement should take place. Freeman et al. (2007, 2010) point to two approaches that an organization and a leader can have to stakeholder engagement, ***managing of stakeholders*** versus ***managing for stakeholders.***

A ***managing of stakeholders*** approach is a so-called ***instrumental*** approach. This means that stakeholder engagement is focused on benefiting the project's interest, even if it may destroy value for the stakeholders. The project manager focuses on getting stakeholders to contribute based on the project's interest. The focus is on those stakeholders who have the most power to influence the project, either positively or negatively. The project manager spends only limited or no resources on stakeholders that the project manager thinks have little or no power to influence the project. The *managing of stakeholders* approach has been criticized for being manipulative and with an ethically incorrect treatment of stakeholders that the organization does not depend on and therefore does not consider important (Freeman et al., 2007).

The criticism is met by a *managing for stakeholders* approach, where the organization, in this case the project, sees each stakeholder as valuable, regardless of their power to influence the project. The focus is on working with stakeholders to create value for both them and the project, as far as possible, without reducing value for either party. This applies to all stakeholders, not just those on whom the project depends (Freeman et al., 2010).

Viewing each stakeholder as valuable is in line with what others have previously suggested, e.g. Donaldson and Preston (1995) and Dill, who wrote as early as 1975:

> For a long time, we have assumed that the views and the initiative of stakeholders could be dealt with as externalities to the strategic planning and management process: as data to help management shape decisions, or as legal and social constraints to limit them. We have been reluctant, though, to admit that some of these outside stakeholders might seek and earn active roles with management to make decisions. The move today is from *stakeholder influence towards stakeholder participation.*
>
> (Dill, 1975, p. 58, emphasis in original)

The *managing for stakeholders* approach has also been criticized, e.g. for being unrealistic (Hahn et al., 2010). It is difficult, and perhaps even impossible, to achieve solutions that provide more value for everyone – and in any case this requires a lot of time and effort, because there are typically conflicts of interest between stakeholders. This means that neither the organization nor the stakeholders achieve (particularly high) additional value (Hahn et al., 2010).

With the current focus on sustainability, the *managing for stakeholders* approach has become widespread. This has led to a change in the language used in connection to stakeholders. This applies both to the general management literature and to the project management literature. In research literature, the term *stakeholder management* is typically no longer used. It has been replaced by *stakeholder engagement*. This is in line with Dill (1975), who, in the above citation, points to a movement from *stakeholder influence* towards *stakeholder participation*.

In this book, we draw on both a *managing of stakeholders* approach and a *managing for stakeholders* approach. It is advantageous to use them in combination, with the aim to create value for all stakeholders while maintaining momentum.

**Mini-case 2 CopenPay – sustainable tourists**

Wonderful Copenhagen is a non-profit organization working to promote and develop tourism in Copenhagen. In the summer of 2024, Wonderful Copenhagen, with inspiration and help from the creative agency Mensch, carried out a project, CopenPay. The project aimed to help brand Copenhagen as a sustainable destination by getting tourists to actively support sustainability.

The project started in the early spring of 2024 when Mensch pitched their project idea for Wonderful Copenhagen. The idea was to let tourism attraction organizations offer tourists to carry out a sustainability task and get a reward in return. The task could be to arrive by bike or on foot, collect garbage in Copenhagen's canals, or help with gardening in an organic vegetable garden. The reward could be an ice cream, a free entry, or a meal.

Wonderful Copenhagen liked the idea, and during May the organization invited a wide range of tourism attraction organizations to offer relevant activities and thus contribute to the project. The organizations would not be paid financially for contributing, but they would get publicity via the marketing campaign for the project and by participating. The project was to be carried out during the high season July–August. For this reason, the invited attraction organizations were only given one week to decide whether they were interested in attending.

Wonderful Copenhagen made agreements with 24 tourism attraction organizations in Copenhagen, e.g. museums and kayak rentals. The project was a huge success. Many tourists participated, and the project received – without having a media budget – overwhelming, international media coverage, with more than 1,400 news articles and reaching over 75 million people.

Mensch and Wonderful Copenhagen even received a marketing award for the project. Perhaps the success of the project will result in similar initiatives in the future by Wonderful Copenhagen or others, in Denmark and abroad.

Sources: Mensch (2024a, 2024b), Obitsø (2024), Terney (2024), and Wonderful Copenhagen (2024a, 2024b)

*The case illustrates how a project, CopenPay, can help an organization, Wonderful Copenhagen, support its purpose, namely to promote and develop tourism in the Capital Region of Denmark. The case also illustrates that a project idea can be generated by a stakeholder outside the base organization, in this case the creative agency Mensch.*

*The case shows that even a short-term project can have many stakeholders, and that some of the stakeholders may already have a relationship with the base organization. This applies, for example, to the tourism attraction organizations that Wonderful Copenhagen invited. It is also worth noting that some stakeholders become very important during the project, such as the international media, and that neither the base organization nor the project has much control over these stakeholders. A media outlet decides for itself what it wants to write about a project and how it wants to angle its story.*

*The case provides insight into how the project can create value for each stakeholder based on their subjective assessment of value, and that the value can be financial or non-financial. Examples include that the tourism attraction organizations get media coverage and more visitors (and thus entrance fees); tourists get an experience and maybe also free admission to an attraction; the City of Copenhagen has garbage collected from the canals; national and international media receive stories and readers or viewers; Mensch receives a client assignment, positive publicity, and a marketing award; and Wonderful Copenhagen and other tourism organizations in Denmark and abroad get an idea for an initiative they can introduce as a recurring activity.*

## References

Chung, K. S. K., Eskerod, P., Jepsen, A. L., & Zhang, J. (2023). Response strategies for community stakeholder engagement on social media: A case study of a large infrastructure project. *International Journal of Project Management*, 41 (5), 102495.

Cleland, D. I. (1985). A strategy for ongoing project evaluation. *Project Management Journal*, 16 (3), 11–17.

Cleland, D. I. (1986). Project stakeholder management. *Project Management Journal*, 17 (4), 36–44.

Dill, W. R. (1975). Public participation in corporate planning – strategic management in a Kibitzer's world. *Long Range Planning*, 8 (1), 57–63.

Di Maddaloni, F., & Davis, K. (2017). The influence of local community stakeholders in megaprojects: Rethinking their inclusiveness to improve project performance. *International Journal of Project Management*, 35 (8), 1537–1556.

Di Maddaloni, F., & Sabini, L. (2022). Very important, yet very neglected: Where do local communities stand when examining social sustainability in major construction projects? *International Journal of Project Management*, 40 (7), 778–797.

Donaldson, T., & Preston, L. E. (1995). The stakeholder theory of the corporation – concepts, evidence, and implications. *Academy of Management Review*, 20 (1), 65–91.

Elkington, J. (2018). 25 years ago I coined the phrase "Triple Bottom Line." Here's why it's time to rethink it. *Harvard Business Review*, 25 June.

Eskerod, P., & Huemann, M. (2024). Project stakeholder orientation principles for managing projects sustainably. In G. Silvius & M. Huemann (Eds.), *Research handbook on sustainable project management* (pp. 240–251). Edward Elgar Publishing.

Freeman, R. E. (1984). *Strategic management: A stakeholder approach.* Pitman.

Freeman, R. E. (1995). Stakeholder thinking: The state of the art. In J. Näsi (Ed.), *Understanding stakeholder thinking* (pp. 35–46). LSR Julkaisu.

Freeman, R. E., Harrison, J. S., & Wicks, A. C. (2007). *Managing for stakeholders: Survival, reputation, and success.* Yale University Press.

Freeman, R. E., Harrison, J. S., Wicks, A. C., Parmar, B. L., & De Colle, S. (2010). *Stakeholder theory: The state of the art.* Cambridge University Press.

Freeman, R. E., Phillips, R., & Sisodia, R. (2020). Tensions in stakeholder theory. *Business & Society*, 59 (2), 213–231.

Freeman, R. E., & Reed, D. L. (1983). Stockholders and stakeholders: A new perspective on corporate governance. *California Management Review*, 25 (3), 88–106.

Gareis, R., Huemann, M., & Martinuzzi, A. (2013). *Project management &sustainable development principles.* Project Management Institute.

Gil, N. A. (2023). Cracking the megaproject puzzle: A stakeholder perspective? *International Journal of Project Management*, 41 (3), 102455.

Hahn, T., Figge, F., Pinkse, J., & Preuss, L. (2010). Trade-offs in corporate sustainability: You can't have your cake and eat it. *Business Strategy and the Environment*, 19 (4), 217–229.

Harrison, J. S., & Wicks, A. C. (2013). Stakeholder theory, value, and firm performance. *Business Ethics Quarterly*, 23 (1), 97–124.

Harrison, J. S., & Wicks, A. C. (2021). Harmful stakeholder strategies. *Journal of Business Ethics*, 169 (3), 405–419.

Huemann, M., & Silvius, A. J. G. (2017). Editorial: Projects to create the future: Managing projects meets sustainable development. *International Journal of Project Management*, 35 (6), 1066–1070.

Ika, L. A., & Pinto, J. K. (2022). The "re-meaning" of project success: Updating and recalibrating for a modern project management. *International Journal of Project Management*, 40 (7), 835–848.

Johnson, G., & Scholes, K. (1993). *Exploring corporate strategy.* Prentice Hall.

King, W. R., & Cleland, D. I. (1978). *Strategic planning and policy.* Van Nostrand Reinhold Company.

Klein, P. G., Mahoney, J. T., McGahan, A. M., & Pitelis, C. N. (2019). Organizational governance adaptation: Who is in, who is out, and who gets what. *Academy of Management Review*, 44 (1), 6–27.

Knutson, J. (2002). *Project management for business professionals: A comprehensive guide.* John Wiley & Sons.

Kujala, J., Sachs, S., Leinonen, H., Heikkinen, A., & Laude, D. (2022). Stakeholder engagement: Past, present, and future. *Business & Society*, 61 (5), 1136–1196.

Locatelli, G., Konstantinou, E., Geraldi, J., & Sainati, T. (2022). The dark side of projects: Dimensionality, research methods, and agenda. *Project Management Journal*, 53 (4), 367–381.

Locatelli, G., Sainati, T., & Mignacca, B. (2024). The dark side of projects: Corruption, sexism, modern slavery, money laundering, inefficient use of resources, and waste of existing assets. In G. Silvius & M. Huemann (Eds.), *Research handbook on sustainable project management* (pp. 97–113). Edward Elgar Publishing.

Mendelow, A. L. (1981). Environmental Scanning: The Impact of the Stakeholder Concept. Proceedings for the International Conference on Information Systems, ICIS 1981. Cambridge, Massachusetts.

Mendelow, A. L. (1983). Setting corporate goals and measuring organizational effectiveness – A practical approach. *Long Range Planning*, 16 (1), 70–76.

Mensch (2024a). Visit Copenhagen CopenPay – casefilm. YouTube video published 11 November. https://www.youtube.com/watch?v=vpU2gor59Cs.

Mensch (2024b). Visit Copenhagen – CopenPay. Copenhagen attractions for climate friendly actions. YouTube video published 7 August. https://www.youtube.com/watch?v=SzOBuMnL-I8.

Obitsø, O. (2024). *Dansk turisme-kampagne tog verden med storm: Nu vinder de Månedens Kampagne* [Danish tourism campaign took the world by storm: Now they win the Campaign of the Month]. Web article published 9 September. https://markedsforing.dk/artikler/nyheder/dansk-turisme-kampagne-tog-verden-med-storm-nu-vinder-de-maanedens-kampagne/.

Rhenman, E. (1964). *Företagsdemokrati och företagsorganisation* [Corporate democracy and corporate organization]. Thule.

Rhenman, E. (1968). *Industrial democracy and industrial management: A critical essay on the possible meanings and implications of industrial democracy.* Van Gorcum.

Rhenman, E. (1973). *Managing the community hospital: Systems analysis of a Swedish hospital.* Saxon House.

Signori, S., & Fassin, Y. (2023). Family members' salience in family business: An identity-based stakeholder approach. *Journal of Business Ethics*, 183 (1), 191–211.

Silvius, A. J. G., & Schipper, R. (2014). Sustainability in project management: A literature review and impact analysis. *Social Business*, 4 (1), 63–96.

Starik, M. (1994). Essay by Mark Starik: The Toronto conference: Reflections on stakeholder theory. *Business & Society*, 33 (1), 89–95.

Terney, S. E. (2024). *Mensch-idé gav København global medieomtale for trecifret mio-beløb* [Mensch-idea gave Copenhagen global media coverage worth three-digit million]. Web article published 16 August. https://markedsforing.dk/artikler/nyheder/mensch-ide-gav-koebenhavn-medieomtale-for-trecifret-mio-beloeb/.

Vuorinen, L., & Martinsuo, M. (2019). Value-oriented stakeholder influence on infrastructure projects. *International Journal of Project Management*, 37 (5), 750–766.

WCED (1987). Report of the World Commission on Environment and Development. https://digitallibrary.un.org/record/139811?v=pdf.

Wonderful Copenhagen (2024a). *Copenhagen launches new green experience economy initiative*, CopenPay. Web article published 8 July. https://www.wonderfulcopenhagen.com/wonderful-copenhagen/international-press/copenhagen-launches-new-green-experience-economy-initiative-copenpay.

Wonderful Copenhagen (2024b). https://www.wonderfulcopenhagen.dk/. Accessed 10 August 2025.

# 3 The basic elements

Project stakeholder engagement requires knowledge about projects, their possible influence on stakeholders, and the contributions that a project needs from the stakeholders. This chapter therefore presents core concepts from project management literature and explains the role of the organization that establishes the project. It also explains value creation and how side effects might influence stakeholders. And it explains the concept of contributions that the projects need from stakeholders and how their expectations influence their willingness to contribute. The chapter concludes with a short presentation of the elements in the stakeholder analysis, which is the topic of the four ensuing chapters.

## Basic building blocks

The project takes place in a *project organization*, which is established by one (or more) organization(s) (*the base organization*). The project generates *deliverables*, e.g. a product or a process that, when implemented, can create value. The total range of deliverables that the project plans to generate is the project *scope*. The purpose of establishing a project is first and foremost to create value for the base organization (Andersen, 2018). The project organization consists in its basic form of a project owner, a project manager, and a project team. The *project owner* personifies the base organization and, with input from others in the base organization, makes the decisions that shape the project. The decisions include, for example, the scope and timeframe of the project and which departments or individuals will deliver which resources to the project.

The project organization is *temporary*. It starts with the project and is dissolved when the project is completed. The project organization

DOI: 10.4324/9781003712695-3

can be expanded with several units, e.g. a steering group and one or more reference groups, and it can also have a parallel project organization in a customer's base organization. It is too extensive to describe the many possible organizational constellations here, and therefore we refer to the basic form throughout the book (with project owner, project manager, and project team).

*Formal project success* is assessed on two dimensions. The first dimension is whether the project is completed within the classic *project triangle*: on time, within budget, and to the agreed specifications. The second dimension concerns whether the deliverables generated by the project, *create the planned value*. A project may well be successful, even if it is *not formally successful*. This can happen if the project becomes much more expensive than planned but succeeds in creating the desired value, and the base organization accepts that the project triangle for various reasons could not be met. A project may be deemed successful even if it neither generates the planned value nor meets the criteria in the project triangle. This can be the case if the project has brought something positive that some stakeholders value, e.g. new knowledge that can be utilized in other settings. At the other end, a project can be considered a *failure, even if it is formally successful*. This typically happens if the project has destroyed much value, e.g. if the project process has required long working days or given significant stress.

A project is, as mentioned, temporary. It has *explicit start- and end-points*. This means that your stakeholder engagement also has a limited duration. It starts with the project, and it has a natural end, even though the stakeholders and you may have relationships and interactions in other contexts and thus interact before and after the project.

But when does the project begin? And when does it end in a stakeholder context? The project can be seen as a sequence of *project management phases*. The *project life cycle* is the time the project runs. The *project investment life cycle* is the entire time during which resources are spent on the project and during which the project generates the planned value and perhaps long-term side effects. The investment life cycle includes a *pre-project* and a *post-project phase* (Gareis et al., 2013). It is important to consider the entire project investment life cycle when identifying stakeholders.

The management phases in the project life cycle are as follows: initiation, planning, implementation, and closure (Andersen, 2018). Figure 3.1 shows a classic project life cycle with its project investment life cycle.

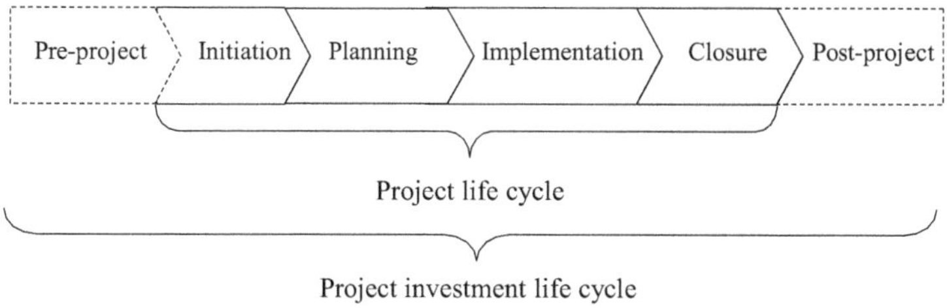


*Figure 3.1* The project life cycle with management phases and the project investment life cycle

The tasks in relation to the project stakeholders vary over the project investment life cycle. In the *pre-project phase*, the project has not yet started, but significant stakeholders, such as a customer and the project owner, are often already involved in the project. Ideally, the base organization, as a preparation for the project, carries out an initial stakeholder analysis, which the project manager can build on.

In the *initiation phase*, the project is established. The project manager is appointed, and the project team formed. Also, the project's budget, timeframe, and specifications for deliverables as well as how these can help create the planned value are decided. This means that focus is on clarifying the project's purpose and on articulating this. In this phase, you should prioritize building relationships between the project and important stakeholders. In this way, you establish the foundation for further collaboration with the stakeholders. To get a good basis for the initial activities that you need to implement in relation to the stakeholders, you should do a stakeholder analysis in this phase.

In the *planning phase*, the project typically has become more well-defined. Therefore, you will be able to identify stakeholders who were not obvious and therefore may not have been identifiable in the initiation phase. An important task is to collaborate with stakeholders who have the knowledge needed to plan the project. Another important task is to align stakeholder expectations. Finally, it is important to make relevant stakeholders aware that the project exists and why, before the project is implemented.

In the *implementation phase*, the relationships created must be maintained, and they must be used when solving the challenges that arise as deviations from the plan occur. The dynamics of the project environment influence the need for active stakeholder engagement in this phase. A very dynamic environment typically results in more deviations from the plan requiring interaction with the stakeholders (Clegg et al., 2024).

Future users are often important stakeholders in this phase, possessing information about product features of importance to them. They must be willing to spend resources testing products and giving information at a time when it is uncertain whether and in what way their contributions will provide value for them. Therefore, it is important that they have confidence that the planned value will come, even though the project organization cannot follow up on this as it comes after the project organization has been dissolved and the project closed. This means that it is important to create a trustful relationship with these stakeholders in this phase.

In the *closure phase*, many stakeholders no longer have an interest in the project (their influence ends). Therefore, you should end relationships in this phase. Some stakeholders remain stakeholders because they are still influenced by or can influence the project. For example, users are still stakeholders after the project ends.

In the *post-project phase*, most projects need the continued contribution of some stakeholders for the deliverables to generate the planned value, e.g. that users use a newly developed product as intended. At this point, the project is closed, and you are no longer working on the project. Therefore, you need to consider in advance how you will ensure that stakeholders contribute during this phase. This may be by involving future stakeholders in the base organization of the project. A long-term perspective is crucial to achieving the planned value.

The explicit timeframe can influence how you think about stakeholders. It can be tempting to think short-term: "We only need this supplier for this one project, so we can afford to pressure him on the price". Thinking about the engagement of a stakeholder short-term and only from the interests of the project can challenge the relationship with the stakeholder, which often extends beyond the individual project. It is therefore better to focus on *creating positive, equal relationships* with stakeholders.

Table 3.1 summarizes characteristics and important tasks in the project management phases.

*Table 3.1* Stakeholder engagement in the project management phases

| | *Initiation* | *Planning* | *Implementation* | *Closure* |
|---|---|---|---|---|
| Characteristics | Little knowledge among both project manager and stakeholders<br>The project budget, timeframe, and specifications are determined | Knowledge is needed for planning<br>The project is about to start, so it needs attention | There are deviations from the plan – how many depends on, among other things, the environmental dynamics<br>Potential future users are often important | The relationships need to be ended |
| Important tasks | Initial stakeholder analysis<br>Stakeholder engagement begins | Further analysis of stakeholders<br>Engaging with stakeholders with needed knowledge<br>Reconcile expectations and negotiate resources and other constraints | Maintain relationships<br>Use relationships when solving problems<br>Involve users if necessary | Create activities to ensure that the relationships end well<br>Engage stakeholders in the base organization to follow up on value realization |

## The project and the base organization

The base organization is an important stakeholder. The base organization influences the project directly and indirectly. It has ***direct influence*** because it establishes the project and allocates resources to the project. Resources are, for example, the employees who will be the project manager and work in the project team. Materials, equipment and facilities are also important resources. The same applies to expertise from departments in the organization, such as knowledge on finance or marketing. Other resources may be needed to ensure that employees in the base organization can create value by using the project's deliverables. This may, for example, be training new work procedures or giving information about the properties of a new product as a basis for selling it.

*Indirect influence* from the base organization happens through organizational culture, processes, and ways of working, including established practices for project management, assignment of project roles, such as project owner, ways of interacting with stakeholders, and norms and values. This means that you need to be aware how project management and other things play out in the base organization. You also need to be aware whether you are subject to any common guidelines for implementing projects. The same applies if the project includes other organizations, e.g. a customer.

The organizational structure influences how complex it is to conduct project stakeholder engagement. *Project-organized* organizations are structured around projects. They typically have many delivery projects for customers. These projects have many similarities. Therefore, the project work, including stakeholder engagement, is systematized. It is more complex to carry out stakeholder engagement in organizations that are instead ***organized into departments with different functions*** (e.g. marketing, finance). Such organizations mostly use projects to implement different types of development, e.g. product or process development, or organizational changes. Projects in such an organization typically share only a few common features with previous projects. In addition, the project manager and the members of the project team are often less experienced in project work than they are in a project-organized organization.

If the base organization is inexperienced in running projects, or there is no experience to draw on from similar projects, it is extra important that you, as a project manager, allocate time to develop well-structured processes for stakeholder engagement. This ensures that you carry out the engagement in a targeted and stable way, and that you can justify your actions. This prevents you from spending unnecessary time on unimportant stakeholders or on sorting out threads due to disappointed expectations.

The base organization not only influences the project; it is also influenced by it. Projects take up resources that could have been used for other projects, and a project may even be designed to change the base organization. This means that stakeholders in the base organization are not necessarily positive towards the project and may need attention to contribute as needed.

Box 3.1 summarizes why the base organization is an important stakeholder for all projects.

**Box 3.1 The base organization as a project stakeholder**

- The base organization establishes the project, defines its purpose, and delimits the project
- The base organization, represented by the project owner, provides the project resources
- The line managers of the members of the project team members are important stakeholders
- The culture of the base organization influences the project work and, therefore, stakeholder engagement
- Projects, including their stakeholder engagement, may be subject to common guidelines
- How the base organization is organized as well as its experience with projects impacts stakeholder engagement
- The base organization is influenced by the project

## Value and side effects

Projects are established to generate *value* for the base organization. Value can be *financial* or *non-financial*. The type of desired value depends on the type of project. In an *internal development project*, also called a *change project*, the purpose is to create a valuable development in the base organization, e.g. through restructuring or process development (Andersen, 2018). This development can then result in financial progress. In a *customer project*, which can be in the form of a *delivery project* or a *development project*, the purpose is to create a product or a service for the customer, which will result in financial value in the base organization through the customer's payment for the deliveries. Customer projects can also create non-financial value for the organization, e.g. by strengthening its reputation, by creating learning that can be used in other projects, or by creating the foundation for new purchase agreements.

Value for the base organization and for each stakeholder can be created (or destroyed) at different times throughout the project process or by the project's deliverables. The project's *deliverables* are generated and delivered during the project or in connection with its completion. The value of *implementing* the generated deliverables usually only appears when the project is completed. An example is a project where the main deliverable is a new school building. It is only when the school building is put into use that the value is created, e.g. in the form of the students learning in a better way. Another example is a project where the main deliverable is a new product line in a company. The value is only created when the company starts to sell the new products to their customers. Similarly, a hospital can initiate the use of a new method for mammography screening to increase capacity. The project deliverable is the new method. It creates value for the hospital by being used.

Most projects *not only result in the planned value*; they also result in *side effects*, which can be negative as well as positive, and thus destroy value or create unplanned value. The term side effect signals that the effect is not part of the value that the project manager is working to create, but something that occurs alongside the planned value creation. Side effects can occur during the project process and after the project is closed.

A construction project can make noise as a *negative side effect*, which can annoy the neighbours and thus diminish their quality of life. It can also result in stress, and perhaps even burnout, for the members of the project team. The annoyance that the neighbours experience will disappear when the project is finished. It is a temporary side effect. The stress and burnout effects are perhaps permanent. They can extend far into the future and may not become apparent until long after the project is finished. The same is the case for other side effects, such as pollution of the surrounding environment. There may also be *positive side effects.* These provide value to stakeholders and give them a reason to contribute to the project. For example, builders may plan to replace an old, shabby house with a new house. This has the positive side effect that the new house will be nicer to look at than the old house, providing value to neighbours and others passing by the house.

Figure 3.2 shows an example of a project that will deliver a factory building with the aim of creating value in the form of increased earnings for the customer. While the construction is ongoing, it has the negative side effect of making noise and disturbing traffic. At the same time, it has the positive side effect of creating additional jobs in the project. Citizens in the local area are important stakeholders, and so is the local job centre. When the factory building is delivered, it has the positive side effect of creating jobs at the factory. It also has the possible negative side effect of making the area less attractive than it was before. Here, the local citizens can again be important stakeholders. They may be able to help give the building an appearance that they think is nice to look at.

You need to *be aware of expected side effects*, especially negative ones, because they can be harmful to the stakeholders, and because they can

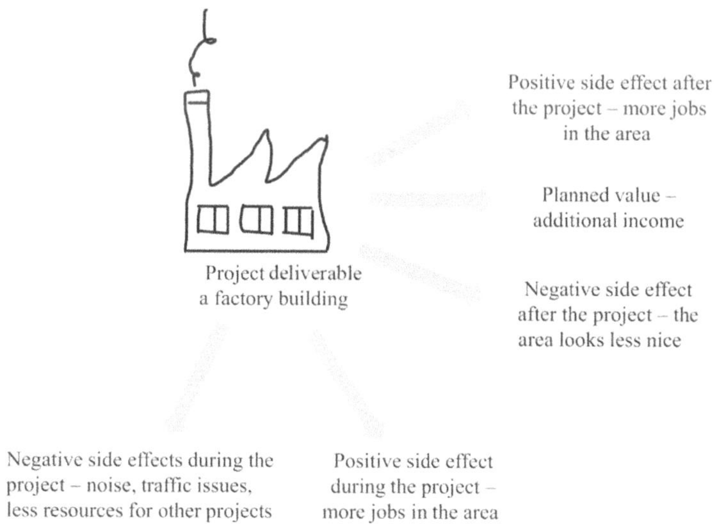


*Figure 3.2* Example of planned value and side effects

deter them from contributing to the project. Negative side effects may even motivate stakeholders to work against the project to avoid or reduce a negative impact. Considering how negative side effects can influence stakeholders and whether you can mitigate them should always be included in stakeholder engagement. Also, be aware that there may be legislation or organizational guidelines (e.g. a code of conduct or a sustainability strategy) that require you to consider possible side effects influencing stakeholders in certain ways in certain situations.

Stakeholders may have very *different views on the value creation* of the project. Perhaps some stakeholders feel that a project, which the base organization sees as successful, has destroyed value for them, because the good results of the project fail to compensate for their loss of value. For example, a flood dyke works as planned, but some of the landowners think that they have been insufficiently compensated for their loss of scenic view – and maybe even think that it is impossible to compensate for this loss. It may also be that a hospital is successful in streamlining some workflows, but some nurses think that the price, reduced patient contact, is too high.

Research has indicated that *is it often possible to create more value than what was expected* at the time of the project's establishment and in the project's business case. You can aim at doing so by consciously working with opportunities that are unknown when the project is established, but which you actively look out for along the way (see, e.g. Lechler et al., 2012, 2013; Eskerod et al., 2018). In a stakeholder context, this implies that the interactions that are part of the stakeholder engagement can be used to acquire knowledge on the stakeholder's needs and wishes, and thereby to develop a better solution for all.

Box 3.2 provides an overview of important issues in relation to the value and side effects of a project.

### Box 3.2 Value and side effects

- The project is established to create value for the base organization
- The project can have positive and negative side effects
- Stakeholders are influenced differently by the project and by its side effects
- The value of the project is different for the base organization and the stakeholders, and it differs across stakeholders

## Contributions and expectations

To create the planned value, the project needs contributions from stakeholders. Stakeholders can contribute financially or in other ways. Examples of contribution in ways other than financial are work effort, knowledge sharing or approvals. Contribution can also occur when decision-makers in the base organization or the authorities provide guidelines, e.g. for requirements for applications, or when suppliers deliver the agreed goods at the agreed time. It is also a contribution when users of the project deliverables, be it a building, a product, new processes, or something else, use the deliverables in a way so that they create the value that is the purpose of establishing the project.

The above are all examples where contribution occurs as a result of the stakeholder *providing something* for the benefit of the project. A stakeholder can also contribute by *refraining from doing something* that will harm the project. For example, some citizens in the project's local area that are against the project could refrain from filing a complaint. It could also be a line manager who refrains from sending his weakest employee to a project team, even though he desires to do so, or a neighbour deciding not to object to a construction project, even though the building will be tall enough to cause annoyance.

Figure 3.3 illustrates that the project influences the stakeholder positively and/or negatively. The stakeholder can contribute or not. The figure also shows that a given action in the project influences more stakeholders than the stakeholder in focus.

Contributing incurs *costs* for the stakeholder, as it requires the use of financial, time, mental, and emotional resources. Often, a stakeholder has alternative uses for the required resources. Therefore, it is important to consider how and to what extent it is necessary for the stakeholder to contribute, so that you draw on the stakeholder's resources as little as possible.

The stakeholder will only contribute if he or she is *motivated* or *forced* to do so. The best way is usually for the stakeholder to contribute based on motivation, which is *an urge to act* to achieve or avoid something. To be motivated, the stakeholder must *expect a benefit* from contributing that is *at least equivalent* to the stakeholder's *costs* of contributing, leading to a gain in value. Some stakeholders benefit directly from using the project's deliverables. This applies, for example, to stakeholders who receive a financial compensation for

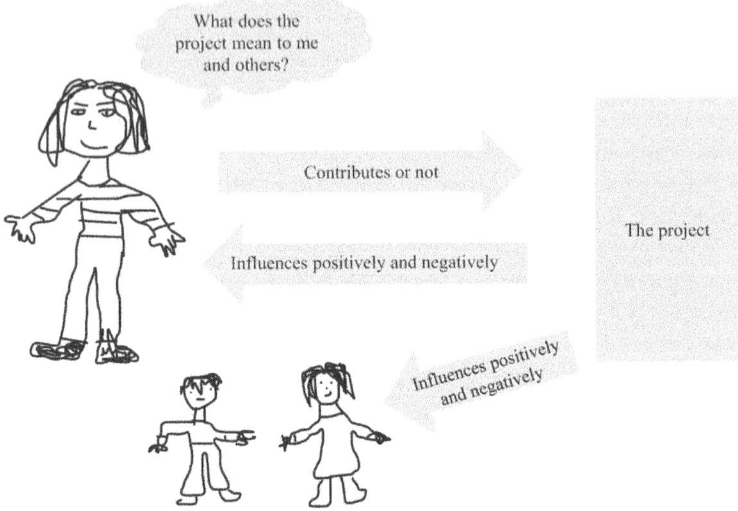


*Figure 3.3* Stakeholder contributions and influences

contributing, e.g. a supplier who receives payment for their goods. This is also the case for a customer who expects to get something out of using the deliverable.

You must *compensate* the stakeholder *in other ways* if direct payments, using the deliverable, or positive side effects do not compensate a stakeholder sufficiently for a contribution. This can be in the form of influence on the project process or the project's deliverables by, e.g. involvement in decision processes, or by being heard in another way, such as at a town hall meeting. Finally, it can be in the form of attention, e.g. by being continually informed.

Whether a stakeholder will contribute may be *more than* a matter of *either contributing or not*. The stakeholder may be willing to *contribute*, but not *sufficiently*. You may need your project owner to give a speech about the project's purpose at an awareness raising event for the project. The project owner may be willing to come to the meeting, but not to give a speech. Perhaps the project owner is only willing to talk informally with the participants about the project's purpose. In this case, you should consider if it is really necessary for the project owner to give the speech – maybe talking to people at the event is sufficient, or someone else can make the speech. If the project owner must make the speech, you need to find out how you can convince the project owner to do so. Another example is a supplier who is willing to deliver a necessary part to the project. But the supplier may not be able or willing to do so by the date when the project needs the part – at least not without financial compensation for the extra costs of delivering faster than standard.

The stakeholders cannot know the future, and therefore they cannot know the actual value from contributing to the project when deciding (not) to do so. This means that they must *assess the value that they will get out of contributing* based on their *expectations.* This makes expectations an important factor in the stakeholders' consideration of contributing to the project.

Expectations can *arise in many ways.* They can arise from formally learned knowledge or from experiences that are generalized to the current situation. Experiences can be relevant but are not always so. The stakeholder may have experiences with similar projects or with working with some of the persons participating in the current project. But maybe the memories or the interpretation of the experience is incorrect, or the experience may not be generalizable to the current situation due to differences. For example, a stakeholder does not want to contribute to this project because of the stakeholder's bad experiences with a similar project. But she may not know the full reason why the previous project went wrong, and she may not have understood that the current project will be implemented in a different way. The same situation applies to positive experiences that are also only generalizable to a limited extent.

Figure 3.4 shows two important dimensions in how expectations influence the willingness to contribute and what you need to work with in the four different situations that result.

In situation (1), the stakeholder is *not willing to contribute* because the stakeholder expects to *get very little out of it, and this is correct.* For example, a supplier may, in line with reality, expect to get a low price for their deliveries. Another example is a stakeholder who, also in line with reality, does not expect to have any influence on the project. In the two examples, the project fails to offer enough for the stakeholder to contribute. The stakeholders are aware of this and are not willing to contribute. This means that you need to *negotiate* or *offer greater value* to motivate the stakeholder to contribute. Negotiations

| Expected value from contributing \ The value that the project will provide for contribution | Low | High |
|---|---|---|
| Low | (1)<br>The stakeholder is not willing to contribute<br>The project must offer larger value, or the value be negotiated | (2)<br>The stakeholder is not willing to contribute<br>Expectations must be aligned, e.g. by informing about actual value |
| High | (3)<br>The stakeholder is willing to contribute<br>Risk of disappointed expectations<br>Expectations must be aligned | (4)<br>The stakeholder is willing to contribute<br>Gets expected value<br>No adjustment needed |

*Figure 3.4* The influence of expectation on wanting to contribute

provide an opportunity to air views and align expectations. This applies both to what the stakeholder finds is a fair compensation for the wanted contributions and what the project can offer the stakeholder. Negotiations can also give insight into the concerns that the stakeholder may have in relation to any negative side effects from the project process or the project's deliveries.

In situations (2) and (3), the stakeholder's expectations differ from the value that the stakeholder gets out of contributing. In this case, you need to *align expectations* with the stakeholder. In situation (2), the stakeholder is *not willing to contribute* because the stakeholder has *too low an expectation* of the value that the stakeholder will get from contributing. Maybe a department manager is reluctant to allocate an employee to a project because the department manager believes that the tasks are boring routine tasks that take many hours. Perhaps this is not the case. This means that it will help the project if expectations reflect reality as much as possible.

In situation (3), the stakeholder is *willing to contribute*. However, this is based on a *too positive expectation* of the value that the stakeholder gets out of contributing. For example, a department manager may send his best employee to the project because the department manager expects that it will give the employee some exciting work tasks. But perhaps the tasks are routine. In this situation you also a need to align expectations to prevent misunderstandings and even breaches of trust if some stakeholders feel that their agreements or expectations are not being met.

In situation (4), the stakeholder is *willing to contribute* based on an expectation of a fair value from contributing, and this is *in line with reality*. This means that there is no need for action.

There are only *limited resources for stakeholder engagement*. Therefore, you need to prioritize. You need to make strategic decisions about how you will engage with the project's stakeholders so that you use the resources most effectively to ensure the needed contribution. You should *prioritize the stakeholders* so that you spend the most resources on those who are need attention to be motivated to contribute as desired, or who are influenced by the project in a very negative way. This means that you should try to predict which stakeholders are sufficiently motivated to contribute, which stakeholders you need to work with to motivate them to contribute, and which stakeholders are influenced so negatively that you should include their interests even if they haven't come forward with them yet. In this regard, it is important that you are aware that each stakeholder has their own interests in and expectations about the project, and you need to take these into account.

It can be a *challenging* task to uncover stakeholder expectations *early in the project*, because you don't know the project or the possible stakeholders. At the same time, your time to create the knowledge is limited at the beginning of the project, because you have many other tasks to perform at this point. This means that you do not have a clear picture of what is needed, as you need to build this knowledge as part of the project. You should therefore *align expectations in an ongoing process* as you get to know more about the project and the stakeholders. Ongoing alignment of expectations is especially necessary when there are many unique elements in the project, which limits the possibility to generalize from other projects.

A particular challenge in expectation alignment is that expectations are often neither clear nor persistent. They are often *implicit* – and perhaps even *unconscious* – and they may well *change* over the course of the project. This is a challenge for the project manager, but also for the stakeholders when expectations must be aligned and agreements must be made.

Box 3.3 displays the main aspects of stakeholder contributions.

**Box 3.3 Aspects of stakeholder contributions**

- The project needs contributions from the stakeholders
- Stakeholders can contribute by acting in favour of the project, by providing financial or other resources such as work time, expertise, or materials
- Stakeholders can contribute by refraining from acting to harm the project
- Contributing to the project involves costs for the stakeholders, e.g. financial, time, mental, and emotional resources
- Stakeholders expect to get something out of their contributions, e.g. financial or other benefits, like positive experiences or attention
- Stakeholders' motivation to contribute is based on expectations about the project and their contributions
- Stakeholders' expectations may be unclear, even to themselves, and they may change
- Stakeholders' expectations can be aligned through ongoing dialogue and negotiation

## A complex task

Every project starts as a new organization and therefore has its own stakeholders. The *relationships with the stakeholders are new and temporary*. This is true even if you know the persons, entities, and organizations involved intimately from other contexts. You have a short time to build a relationship with the stakeholders, and everyone knows from the start that it is temporary.

Stakeholder interaction is complicated by the fact that *each issue has its own stakeholders*. In addition, stakeholders may have different levels of interest in different issues. For example, department heads involved in appointing team members will be interested in team formation but may not be interested in the project's use of social media. Another example is future users of the deliverables. They are particularly interested in a product development project when it reaches the testing phase.

Stakeholder engagement is also complicated by the fact that *the project stakeholders also have stakeholders* to consider. The project is probably not the only customer for the supplier. Perhaps your supplier uses a subcontractor that you are not entirely satisfied with due to quality issues. If you are a very important customer for the supplier, and the supplier can replace the subcontractor, you may be able to get by with this happening, at least on your project. However, if it is important to the supplier that the subcontractor survives, and thus has many orders to fill, because the subcontractor is important to other customers, you will have to find another way out. You can change to another supplier, but this is often not possible due to contractual conditions. Instead, you may have to initiate direct stakeholder engagement with the supplier's subcontractor to ensure quality.

In some cases, stakeholders must also *represent the interests of others*, such as a company, nature and other non-humans, the municipality, or even future generations. In some cases, this is regulated by law, so that public authorities or others represent the interests of vulnerable stakeholders. For example, they may represent the interests of local citizens in connection with infrastructure projects such as the construction of a motorway. When the stakeholder represents the interests of others, it is difficult for the stakeholder to completely disregard their *own interests*. The stakeholder's personal position towards the project may support or oppose how they represent the interests of others. For example, a representative of a public authority may try to take care of their own working hours. Therefore, the representative may not want to set up as many meetings as the citizens would like.

The above suggests that it is desirable to include considerations about the stakeholder's stakeholders in your stakeholder engagement. However, it may not be possible to do so because you have only limited knowledge about these stakeholders, and you often do not have access to them.

Box 3.4 summarizes the complexities of stakeholder engagement.

**Box 3.4 Complexities in stakeholder engagement**

- The collaborative relationships are new and temporary
- Each project has its own stakeholders
- Each issue in the project has its own stakeholders
- Stakeholders have their own stakeholders

- Stakeholders sometimes represent the interests of other stakeholders
- It can be difficult to disregard own interests when representing other stakeholders

## The stakeholder analysis

Knowledge of (and recognition of) the other party's requirements, wishes, interests, concerns, and preferences, as well as clarity about your own expectations, is a prerequisite for a good collaboration. This also applies to engagement with stakeholders. You therefore need to analyse the stakeholders to succeed with good stakeholder engagement.

The stakeholder analysis contributes to stakeholder engagement in two ways: first, it provides a basis for planning well-thought-out activities in relation to each (group of) stakeholder(s). Second, the activities required to carry out the stakeholder analysis contribute to stakeholder engagement, because collecting the necessary information requires interaction with the stakeholders. This means that the engagement already starts with the data collection.

The project is not clearly delimited at the outset, and detailed plans typically are not yet in place at this point. Therefore, you need to, during the project course, repeatedly enhance the initial stakeholder analysis, which you carry out at the beginning of the project.

There are three essential steps in the stakeholder analysis (inspired by Cleland, 1985; Eskerod & Jepsen, 2016):

- Who are the project stakeholders?
- Does the stakeholder have the intention to contribute as the project needs?
- Which stakeholders should you prioritize giving attention?

The next three chapters cover each of these three questions. In Chapter 7, we provide suggestions on how you can obtain the necessary information for the analysis.

The result of the stakeholder analysis is a *stakeholder register*. We have developed a simple register, which you can see in Table 6.2 and in Appendix B.

**Mini-case 3 Mindvalley U – co-creating with stakeholders**

Events, e.g. conferences, can be considered projects due to their temporary nature and range of stakeholders. Events are characterized by the fact that the duration is fixed. At a conference, the deliverables are presentations that are meant to give the attendees an experience. An important element in the conference experience is also social networking.

The attendees at a conference are stakeholders that can be influenced by the conference activities and venue and the other attendees. They can also influence the conference, e.g. by making a presentation and by mingling with other attendees and speakers.

Mindvalley U is an annual conference organized by Mindvalley, which offers personal transformation globally through online and on-site activities. The first conference took place in Barcelona in 2017. In August 2025, the Mindvalley U conference took place in Amsterdam, supplemented by an option for online attendance.

Mindvalley U offers sessions by invited speakers. In addition, the organizers create room for attendees to apply to become a so-called community speaker. The invited speakers and the community speakers selected for presentations all do their presentations at one of the Mindvalley U venue stages.

Mindvalley U encourages attendees, whose application was not selected for presentation and attendees who have not applied to present, to create and organize their own events outside the conference venue of Mindvalley U, e.g. in a rented space, and to announce the event through an agenda app provided to all attendees. Mindvalley U explicitly states that the off-venue events should be provided free of charge. If money exchange at all is involved, it should only be to cover direct costs, e.g. rental of the venue.

The agenda app contains a current version of the conference agenda, and it allows the attendees to create a profile with photo and bio, to connect with other attendees who have uploaded a profile. It also allows attendees to announce their own off-venue events without any requirements for approval of neither event nor announcement.

During the conference in 2025, Mindvalley U added an extra six-hour event to the agenda for present as well as online attendees, demonstrating the dynamic of the agenda.

The Mindvalley U conference is not only about conducting a successful conference that creates value by giving attendees good experiences. Mindvalley also uses the conference to discover talent, mostly among the community speakers and the off-venue speakers. They invite selected individuals for further cooperation with Mindvalley, e.g. offering a role as a Mindvalley speaker as a later event or an activity at the Mindvalley website.

Sources: Mindvalley (2017, 2018, 2022, 2025a, 2025b)

*Mindvalley U is a project established by the base organization, Mindvalley, to create value for its community through knowledge provision and social networking, and for Mindvalley through talent discovery.*

*The case illustrates how modern technology, like the Mindvalley U agenda app, can enable co-creation of value with stakeholders. By allowing and encouraging all attendees to reach out to each other to organize meetups and to announce own events without an approval process, Mindvalley U demonstrates a clear intent of value co-creation and a desire to embrace a dynamic project scope.*

## References

Andersen, E. S. (2018). *Prosjektledelse – et organisasjonsperspektiv*, 2. utgave [Project management – an organizational perspective, 2nd ed.]. Fagbogforlaget.

Clegg, S. R., Skyttermoen, T., & Vaagaasar, A. L. (2024). *Project management: Creating sustainable value*, 2nd ed. Sage.

Cleland, D. I. (1985). A strategy for ongoing project evaluation. *Project Management Journal*, 16 (3), 11–17.

Eskerod, P., & Jepsen, A. L. (2016). *Project stakeholder management.* Routledge.

Eskerod, P., Ang, K., & Andersen, E. S. (2018). Increasing project benefits by project opportunity exploitation. *International Journal of Managing Projects in Business*, 11 (1), 35–52.

Gareis, R., Huemann, M., & Martinuzzi, A. (2013). *Project management & sustainable development principles.* Project Management Institute.

Lechler, T. G., Edington, B., & Gao, T. (2012). Challenging classic project management: Turning project uncertainties into business opportunities. *Project Management Journal*, 43 (6), 59–69.

Lechler, T. G., Gao, T., & Edington, B. (2013). *The silver lining of project uncertainties.* Project Management Institute.

Mindvalley (2017). A plan to reinvent university: Mindvalley University. YouTube video published 3 March. https://www.youtube.com/watch?v=TW4L14JTToI. Accessed 25 August 2025.

Mindvalley (2018). A new vision for modern education: Welcome to Mindvalley University. YouTube video published 29 March. https://www.youtube.com/watch?v=-czrMKIkdw. Accessed 25 August 2025.

Mindvalley (2022). Mindvalley U: Behind the vision. YouTube video published 19 May. https://www.youtube.com/watch?v=HSTyToGGDA4. Accessed 25 August 2025.

Mindvalley (2025a). What to expect at Mindvalley U 2025. YouTube video published 25 June. https://www.youtube.com/watch?v=yslGVQ_UjEs. Accessed 25 August 2025.

Mindvalley (2025b). Mindvalley x 2025: Breakthrough ideas, future tech & world-class teachers. YouTube video published 9 August. https://www.youtube.com/watch?v=Whmb7UC27xM. Accessed 3 September 2025.

# 4 Who are the stakeholders?

The first element of the stakeholder analysis is to identify and describe the project stakeholders. Important elements in this are the contributions that the project needs from each stakeholder and the stakeholder's ability to influence the project positively and negatively.

## Stakeholder identification

The first task is to identify the project stakeholders. There are several ways of doing this (Eskerod & Jepsen, 2016):

- Consult relevant legislation as well as regulations in the base organization to see if there are requirements for engaging specific stakeholders
- Obtain input from key individuals in the project organization, e.g. the project owner
- Use existing lists of typical stakeholders, e.g. from project management standards in the base organization, or in networks
- Ask project team members to list possible stakeholders within their area of expertise
- Check stakeholder registers from other projects
- Ask stakeholders who have already been identified if they can think of any stakeholders missing from your list
- Invite experts inside or outside the base organization to review your stakeholder list and point out any overlooked stakeholders.

Be aware that *the stakeholder defines* whether he or she is influenced by the project. This especially holds true in relation to expected negative

DOI: 10.4324/9781003712695-4

side effects. You must ensure a fair treatment of all individuals and entities, who feel that they are or will be influenced by the project. This includes individuals who, in your opinion, will not be influenced. To simply reject such views can be dangerous for the project's success. For example, citizens who are bothered by noise from a construction project may join in making a well-founded complaint about the noise. This may result in investigations having to be carried out, stopping the project from progressing. The issue could maybe have been solved by a dialogue with the citizens before starting the works, to learn about their concerns in order to find a way to address them.

The list of stakeholders can quickly become comprehensive, and you risk being *overwhelmed by the number of individuals and entities* that you must consider when working on the project. You can prevent this by deciding to ignore some of the stakeholders. This is, however, a risky way to go because you may end up leaving out stakeholders who are important, either now or in the future.

A better approach is to *aggregate stakeholders in groups* based on relevant characteristics. Typical groupings are investors, the board, employees, suppliers, customers, and end users. There is no golden rule for the appropriate number of groups. It depends on the complexity of the project, but also on the stakeholders that are involved in the project at hand. Some researchers, e.g. Bradley (2006), recommend aiming to work with 6–15 groups.

It is convenient to work with a few large groups. However, be aware that *every individual* involved in the project has their own interests in the project. If an individual stands out from their stakeholder group, it may be relevant to treat this stakeholder differently than the rest of the group. For example, you may see the employees in a department as a group, because they are all influenced by a project in approximately the same way. However, there may be one or more individuals in this group who stand out from the rest, e.g. because they are able to influence other members of the group or have a comparatively large interest in the project. This may be a very experienced employee or one or several very negative employees. Such individuals need more attention than the others in the group. Therefore, it may be relevant to single them out as a separate group in your stakeholder identification or, in other words, to *disaggregate* the employee group.

A need for disaggregating a group may not be clear at the outset of the project. It often materializes as the project progresses. If stakeholders need to be singled out, you must revise the list of stakeholders. Typically, you will need to do that several times during the project, because new information appears, and because things change.

Table 4.1 shows an excerpt from the stakeholder register for a wind turbine project. The customer can influence the project positively by engaging in the development of the project deliverables, and influence negatively by breaking agreements or leaving the project. The customer is influenced by the project through the agreed deliverables. The table also provides examples for two other stakeholders: the head of a development department and a birder.

## Necessary contributions from each stakeholder

The next issue is to establish what the project *at least* needs the stakeholder to do or refrain from doing. This is the *stakeholder's necessary contributions.* This could, for example, involve approving or allocating financial resources to project activities. It could also be allocating employee resources or refraining from speaking negatively about the project. You can use various project documents,

*Table 4.1* Examples of how the project can influence and be influenced by stakeholders

| *Stakeholder* | *Influence on the project* | *Influenced by the project* |
|---|---|---|
| Customer X | Can engage in development of the project deliverables (p)<br>Can break agreements (n)<br>Can leave the project (n) | Gets deliverables from the project (p) |
| Head of development department | Can provide good or bad employee resources to the project (p/n)<br>Can free the members of the project team from other tasks or burden them with other tasks (p/n) | The project draws employee resources from the department (n) |
| Birder | Can attempt to stop the project through protests (n) | Is concerned that birds will be harmed by the project (n) |

Notes: p=positive, n=negative

such as the project's business case, the project mandate or the description of the project's purpose and deliverables to clarify the stakeholder's necessary contributions. Table 4.2 provides examples of necessary contributions to the wind turbine project for the same stakeholders as in Table 4.1.

## The stakeholder's requirements and wishes

Stakeholders are influenced by the project in different ways. Some are influenced positively from the project, while others are negatively influenced. Many experience a bit of both. A stakeholder will only contribute if he or she expects to get a higher benefit than the cost of contributing. The stakeholder's expectations can be indispensable, i.e. in the form of *requirements*, or they can be soft, i.e. in the form of *wishes*. A benefit can, for example, be a payment or influence on decisions, but it can also be in the form of reduced negative side effects.

To help assess how closely the project should meet the stakeholder's requirements and wishes, you can consider how legitimate or urgent these are (Mitchell et al., 1997). Requirements are *legitimate* if the stakeholder will lose much, i.e. be significantly negatively influenced, if you fail to meet them. This means that you, for ethical reasons, should meet a legitimate requirement from a stakeholder, even if this is not in the immediate interest of the project. *Urgency* refers to how time-sensitive a requirement is. If a legitimate requirement is urgent, you should prioritize the stakeholder timewise. A single neighbour to a construction project typically has no or little possibility to influence the project.

*Table 4.2* Examples of stakeholders' necessary contributions

| *Stakeholder* | *Necessary contributions* |
|---|---|
| Customer X | Sign a contract for wind turbine delivery<br>Willing to interact directly with the project |
| Head of development department | Assign two employees for a month to the project team |
| Birder | Trust that the birds will not suffer significant harm<br>Refrain from protesting |

However, if a neighbour, during the project, discovers that the foundation of her house has begun to crack, it is both a legitimate and an urgent requirement to ask you to act on the matter. The legitimacy is that the cracks reduce the value of the neighbour's home, and perhaps also the safety in it. The urgency is that it is possible that the further progress of the project will worsen the cracks. Therefore, action cannot wait.

## Stakeholders' ability to influence the project

How much a stakeholder can influence the project depends on the stakeholder's *power*, as we mentioned in Chapter 2, when presenting Mendelow's matrix. Power can be the potential to *influence the project positively* – i.e. to help the project – or it can be a potential to *influence the project negatively*, thereby threatening its success – i.e. to harm the project (Savage et al., 1991). The two types of power are not opposites; they complement each other.

Stakeholders who have many resources, e.g. money, working hours, expertise, facilities, or moral support, have the potential to positively influence the project by providing resources for the project. Stakeholders who can stop the project or hinder its progress, e.g. by withholding resources, not using the project's deliverables as planned, or by damaging the project's image, have the potential to negatively influence the project (Nguyen et al., 2020). The more dependent the project is on a stakeholder, the greater the stakeholder's ability to influence the project negatively.

Stakeholders have a large or a small potential to influence the project, and they can influence it positively or negatively. This gives a total of four possible stakeholder categories, which we, inspired by Savage et al. (1991), Ackermann and Eden (2011), and Eskerod and Jepsen (2016), have labelled: *key player*, *resourceful*, *showstopper*, and *marginal*.

*Key players* are stakeholders who have power to influence the project both positively *and* negatively. This applies, for example, to a stakeholder who controls important resources that others cannot provide. The stakeholder can influence the project positively by providing the resources for the project. The stakeholder can also influence the project negatively by withholding the resources. An example of such a stakeholder is a supplier who is the only one who can supply a given component.

A *resourceful* stakeholder can influence the project positively but not negatively. This applies to a stakeholder who has important resources that other stakeholders can also provide. It can, for example, be two suppliers that can both assume the role of main supplier. They each have a high potential to positively influence the project, but little potential to negatively influence the project.

The *showstopper* is a stakeholder who can negatively influence the project by obstructing or even stopping it, but who cannot help the project. An example is a governmental agency that can stop a project that does not comply with the legislation (i.e. they have authority), but who cannot give resources or in other ways influence the project positively.

The last stakeholder category, the *marginal*, has little or no ability to positively or negatively influence the project. Therefore, this stakeholder is of marginal importance from the project's perspective. It is important to remember that you should not simply ignore *marginal* stakeholders. Even though they lack the power to influence the project, they are stakeholders, if they can be influenced by the project process, its deliverables, or its side effects.

Figure 4.1 illustrates the categorization.

You can use a scenario technique (Wack, 1985) to assess the potential of a stakeholder to positively or negatively influence the project by imagining *the best of all worlds* for a stakeholder's involvement to assess the potential to positively influence the project, or *the*

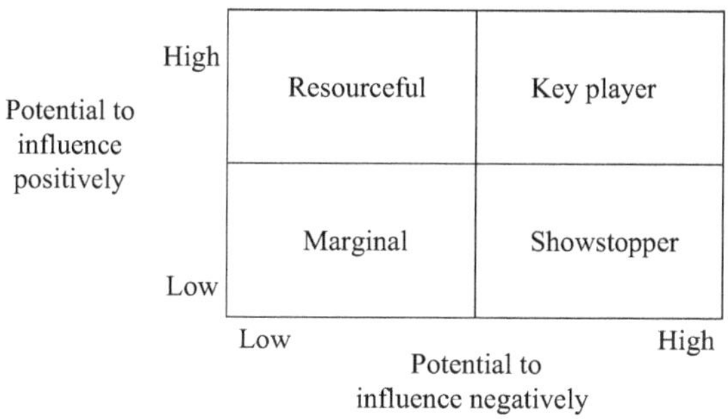


*Figure 4.1* Stakeholders' potential to influence positively and negatively
Sources: Inspired by Savage et al. (1991), Ackermann and Eden (2011), and Eskerod and Jepsen (2016)

*worst of all worlds* to assess a stakeholder's potential to negatively influence the project by imagining the stakeholder's behaviour towards the project. Some questions can help with stakeholder assessment (Savage et al., 1991):

- Does the stakeholder possess resources that are necessary for project implementation?
- Is it likely that the stakeholder will take action to influence the project positively or negatively?
- Is the stakeholder likely to network with other stakeholders? With members of the project team? With other individuals?

The last question emphasizes that you, when assessing a stakeholder's power, need to consider that stakeholders often share interests with other stakeholders and may have access to powerful individuals. Stakeholders who share interests can form a coalition. Individuals can build credibility and legitimacy around their requirements by showing that several others share their point of view (Nguyen et al., 2020). By joining forces, they gain more resources to engage in a potential conflict.

If you believe that *a stakeholder shares an interest with others* or *has access to powerful stakeholders*, you can benefit from drawing up a *stakeholder network* (Ackermann & Eden, 2011). Figure 4.2 shows such a network. The stakeholder in focus is placed in the middle. The stakeholder's network is placed around the stakeholder. The network contains two types of stakeholders. The first type of stakeholder belongs to *the interest base*. These are individuals or entities who perceive *being influenced* by the project in the same way as the stakeholder in focus – or at least in a similar way. The second type of stakeholder belongs to *the power base*, which contains stakeholders who strengthen the stakeholder's potential to influence the project. These are individuals or entities with power in relation to the project – who can influence it – and *whom the stakeholder can activate to influence* the project.

In Figure 4.2, we see an example of a stakeholder network with the power base at the top of the figure and the interest base at the bottom. The example focuses on an employee in a department, which is to initiate a digital transformation project. The employee has an interest in the project, because the employee is required to participate

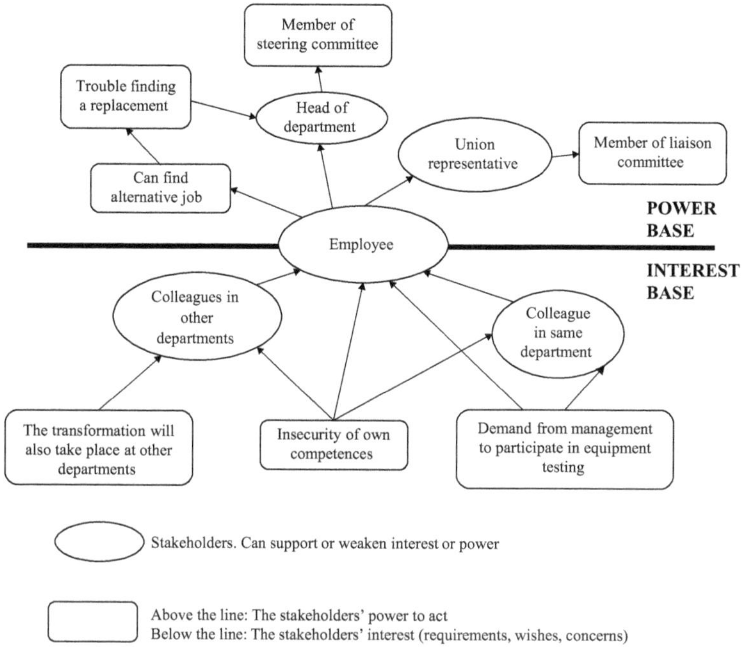


*Figure 4.2* Example of a stakeholder network
Source: Inspired by Ackermann and Eden (2011)

in testing new equipment. The employee feels negatively influenced by this, because she is unsure whether she has the necessary skills. The employee discusses her concern with the other employee who is assigned to testing the equipment. The concern is also shared by colleagues in other departments, who anticipate that they may soon be required to use the equipment. Other employees sharing her concerns strengthens the interest base of the employee in focus.

At the top of the figure, we see the employee's power base. It is supported by relationships with other individuals who can influence the project. In this example, the employee is a member of the union, and the union representative is a member of the liaison committee, where work environment challenges are discussed. In addition, the employee works in a field where there is a shortage of labour. Therefore, the employee can relatively easily find another job and will be difficult to replace. This means that the employee has a certain amount of power in relation to the department head, who is a member of the steering committee for the project. The stakeholder can enforce legitimate requirements through these relationships.

## Stakeholder identification in brief

You can identify the stakeholders by considering who can influence or be influenced by the project. Important in consideration of possibility to influence is whether an individual or an entity can contribute with important resources that only they have. Another important element is what they require or wish to receive in exchange for contributing. Remember also that individuals or entities with no power over the project are stakeholders if they are influenced by the project.

**Mini-case 4 Eat the packaging**

The DTU National Food Institute, which develops new and better food by sustainable technological solutions, has received €1.3 million from Innovation Fund Denmark to initiate a research and innovation project that aims at developing an edible food wrap.

The project is carried out with two partners, the Department of Food Science at the University of Copenhagen (UCPH Food) and the company CP Kelgo. UCPH Food are experts in reducing the environmental impact of food production and in consumer preferences in relation to sustainability. CP Kelgo is a global company that develops and produces food ingredients and has expertise in recycling and by-products. The DTU National Food Institute has previously worked with both partners.

The project is planned to take three years to complete. It will deal with the technical development of the wrap and examine food safety issues.

The project description specifies that the wrap must be produced with, among other things, residual products from the juice industry in the form of citrus peels. The project description also specifies that the wrap must be tested as packaging on minced beef, frozen pizza, and portion rice (in a cooking bag). In addition to keeping the food fresh and safe, the wrap must "disappear" during cooking, e.g. in a pan. There are no requirements for the cooking methods which can be used. The wrap must be usable for both private households and professional kitchens, and the project will also examine perception of the wrapping and taste experience through involvement of potential users.

Source: DTU National Food Institute (2023)

*The case illustrates that project stakeholders can have the power to influence the project in different ways.*

*The DTU National Food Institute is the base organization for the project and therefore must facilitate that important decisions are made. Innovation Fund Denmark can supply or withhold financial resources. The DTU National Food Institute has used influential power towards Innovation Fund Denmark to secure financial resources for the project. Now that the resources have been given, Innovation Fund Denmark has become less powerful as long as the project sticks to the agreements for the funding.*

*The partners UCPH Food and CP Kelgo have resources in the form of necessary expertise. The DTU National Food Institute has gained access to this expertise and secured continued access to it by entering a collaboration with the two partners, thereby giving them significant possibility to influence the project.*

*User groups within private households and professional kitchens can influence the project through their willingness to test the wrap during the project process and their willingness to purchase the wrap when the finalized version is available on the market.*

*The case further illustrates how collaborations with stakeholders can extend over several projects, and that collaborations can lead to new, joint projects.*

*The case can help us remember that a project's stakeholders are everyone who can influence or be influenced by the project's deliverables, and that these stakeholders must be considered in both stakeholder analysis and engagement. No matter how good a wrap the project can produce, it will only create significant value if the wrap is accepted by the stakeholders on the product's way to be used by future customers. This applies to those who will produce the wrap, those who will sell the wrap, and those who will buy or use the wrap. The latter can, for example, be end users at home as well as catering kitchen staff. It is, therefore, a good decision that the project will involve consumers so that they can express their perception and taste experience of the wrap.*

## References


Ackermann, F., & Eden, C. (2011). Strategic management of stakeholders: Theory and practice. *Long Range Planning*, 44 (3), 179–196.

Bradley, G. (2006). *Benefit realisation management*. Gower.

DTU National Food Institute (2023). *I fremtiden kan du spise din fødevareemballage* [In the future, you can eat your food packaging]. Web article published 23 November. https://www.food.dtu.dk/nyheder/i-fremtiden-kan-du-spise-din-foedevareemballage?id=46d92c74-c968-47b4-94f2-81fc7a96fc1b.

Eskerod, P., & Jepsen, A. L. (2016). *Project stakeholder management*. Routledge.

Mitchell, R. K., Agle, B. R., & Wood, D. J. (1997). Toward a theory of stakeholder identification and salience: Defining the principle of who and what really counts. *Academy of Management Review*, 22 (4), 853–886.

Nguyen, T. H. D., Chileshe, N., Rameezdeen, R., & Wood, A. (2020). Stakeholder influence strategies in construction projects. *International Journal of Managing Projects in Business*, 13 (1), 47–65.

Savage, G.T., Nix, T. W., Whitehead, C. J., & Blair, J. D. (1991). Strategies for assessing and managing organizational stakeholders. *Academy of Management Perspectives*, 5 (2), 61–75.

Wack, P. (1985). Scenarios: Uncharted waters ahead. *Harvard Business Review*, 63 (5), 73–89.

# 5 Will the stakeholder contribute?

Stakeholder contributions are important for project success. The relationship between the project and each stakeholder is a series of *exchanges*, where both parties give and receive, and where both parties decide whether or not they want to participate in this exchange. It is far from certain that stakeholders will readily see any reason to do so. They may even see a good reason to oppose the project.

To ensure stakeholder contributions, you therefore must understand what the stakeholders think about doing the act needed to contribute. In the following chapter, we look at the stakeholder considering this through the lens of the *theory of planned behaviour* (Ajzen, 1985), which we supplement with the concept of *perception of fairness* (Bosse et al., 2009).

## The theory of planned behaviour

The theory of planned behaviour (Ajzen, 1985) assumes that individuals consciously consider whether to do an act before they do it. In a stakeholder context, the act may, for example, be to support a project by attending a meeting where important decisions are to be made. If an individual decides to do the act, i.e. go to the meeting, we say that the stakeholder has an *intention to act*. According to the theory of planned behaviour, stakeholders base their intention to act on consideration of three aspects.

The first aspect is the *attitude towards doing the act* (in Ajzen's model *attitude towards the behaviour*). This is the stakeholder's consideration of whether he or she will gain value from doing the act. The attitude towards doing the act will be positive if the stakeholder

DOI: 10.4324/9781003712695-5

expects that this will provide value. For example, a stakeholder who considers attending an information meeting about a project will form a positive attitude towards doing so, if she expects that she can influence the project by participating and expressing her opinion.

The second aspect is the *social norm* (in Ajzen's model the *subjective norm*). It is the stakeholder's considerations about what important others will think about him or her doing the act, e.g. whether the stakeholder's manager would find it relevant for the stakeholder to participate in the meeting. The opinion of significant others can strengthen or weaken the intention to act, in our example to participate in the meeting.

The third aspect is the *perceived ability to do the act* (in Ajzen's model *perceived behavioural control*). This element has two parts. First, does the stakeholder believe he or she has the *necessary competences to perform the act*. For example, the stakeholder may think that she lacks the skills to participate in and express an opinion at the meeting. Second, does the stakeholder believe that it is *up to him or her to decide* whether to do the act. It may be that the stakeholder's manager would be the one to decide whether the stakeholder will participate in the meeting.

Figure 5.1 summarizes the influence of the three aspects of the intention to act, which in this context is to perform an act that will contribute to the project.

It is worth noting that individuals form an intention to act (in this case, the act needed to contribute to the project) based on what they find is *sufficient information* to make a *satisfactory choice* instead of pursuing

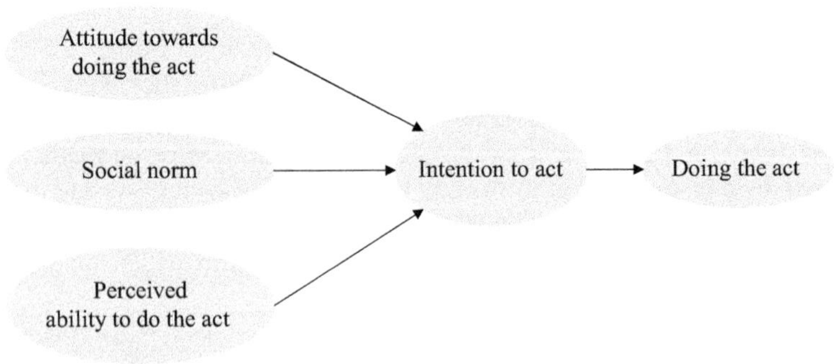


*Figure 5.1* The aspects behind the intention to act
Source: Inspired by Ajzen (1985)

all possible information available. The intention – the conscious decision to act – is therefore based on *bounded rationality* and not on *full rationality*, which would require full information about all alternatives (Simon, 1956). In a project stakeholder context, this means that stakeholders often refrain from seeking or receiving additional information before deciding whether to act or not. This means that it can be challenging to give important information to stakeholders, if they are not aware that it will benefit them. And it is also important to consider that when stakeholders contemplate doing an act, they, as described in Chapter 3, evaluate the three aspects based on *what they expect* is needed from them and what will happen when they do the act.

Before discussing the elements of the theory of planned behaviour in more detail, we need to mention that many acts are carried out without a consciously decided intention to do the act. Instead, they are habitual or impulsive (Ajzen, 1985). With *habitual behaviour*, decisions about acts are based on learned patterns and a – perhaps not reflected – belief that a previously successful behaviour can be generalized to the current situation, wherefore the behaviour can be repeated. For example, it may be the habit to form the project team with one person from production and one from sales plus a few others, instead of purposefully forming the team based on the specific needs of the project at hand. *Impulsive behaviour* occurs as a quick reaction to an impulse. For most individuals, impulsive behaviour occurs when there is time pressure or when very little damage can be done by making a wrong choice.

Projects always contain some degree of novelty, and they often involve decisions with major consequences. Therefore, stakeholders with a high interest in the project generally cannot rely on what they usually do (habits) or simply act impulsively, because it would be too risky. This means that they must make conscious and purposeful decisions about what they want to do – and this in turn means that they consciously form an intention to act before they carry it out.

## Attitude towards doing the act

The first aspect behind the stakeholder's intention to act is the stakeholder's attitude towards doing the act. This attitude is based on two elements. First is the stakeholder's *expected consequence* of performing the act – "what will happen when I do it?" Second is whether the stakeholder sees any *positive or negative value of the consequence* – "do I like what will happen?"

A stakeholder forming an attitude towards doing an act by considering the expected consequence follows a *logic of consequence* (March, 1994). Based on classical economic theory, an intention to act requires that the stakeholder believes that the consequence of doing the act is in his or her *self-interest* (Smith, 1776). To assess whether this is the case, the stakeholder *compares* the expected *benefits* with the expected *costs* of doing the act. Benefits and costs can be in financial or other forms. Benefits can, for example, be that something is nice to do, or that the outcome is positive, such as better working conditions or getting influence. Non-financial costs can, for example, be time, use of mental or emotional capacity, or that the resources that the stakeholder spends on doing the act, such as time, cannot be used for other things.

The stakeholder's consideration of the consequences of contributing involves both *the experience of doing the act* and *what comes out of doing it*. For example, a stakeholder may think that only little will come out of an information meeting, but the stakeholder goes to the meeting anyway because he expects participation to be enjoyable. Another example might be a customer who spends time participating in meetings about a construction project because she believes that a better result will come out of the project if she does so. Figure 5.2 shows a stakeholder considering consequences.

The *magnitude of the benefit* can be the reason for a positive difference between benefits and costs, and thus a positive consequence of doing the act required to contribute. However, a positive consequence may also come from a *low cost* involved in doing the act. This means that a stakeholder who, with a small effort – i.e. with small costs – can contribute and thereby achieve a positive benefit, will be more likely to form a positive attitude towards doing the act needed to contribute than a stakeholder for whom it is difficult – i.e. with large costs. You should therefore think about two aspects when considering how you can create the greatest possible positive consequence for the stakeholder: how you can *increase the benefits*, and how you can *reduce the costs*.

As already mentioned in Chapter 3, the stakeholder does not assess the *actual* consequence of contributing. Instead, the stakeholder assesses the *expected* consequence, which is based on expected benefits

*Figure 5.2* A stakeholder considering expected consequences

and expected costs. This means that it is sometimes more relevant to work with the stakeholder's expectations than to try to give the stakeholder greater benefits or lower costs. Perhaps the stakeholder's attitude towards contributing is negative based on a wrong perception of the consequences. This may be the case, if the assessment is based on incorrect or incomplete information, e.g. based on previous experiences, or a lack of understanding of the project. The attitude can also be negative based on an expectation that a large effort is necessary. Perhaps the effort required is less than expected.

The assessment of the consequence of doing the act, i.e. whether it entails *value*, differs from stakeholder to stakeholder. This is because the stakeholder attaches greater or lesser value to the consequence based on his or her *preferences* – what the stakeholder likes or dislikes. One person may greatly appreciate the city getting a new museum, while another person is completely indifferent. Preferences also apply to doing the necessary acts. One person may perceive a task as fun to perform, while another person perceives the same task as unpleasant. The two persons may have the same perception of what the task entails, but they feel differently when it comes to whether it is fun or unpleasant to do it. For example, one person will perceive going on a business trip, with hotel stays and dinners, as positive because the person likes to stay in a hotel and eat in a restaurant. Another person may not like hotel stays and dinners and will therefore have a negative attitude towards going on the trip. It is important to note that the perception of a task as difficult does not necessarily imply a negative attitude towards doing the act. It depends entirely on personal preferences. Some may find it more rewarding to tackle a difficult challenge than an easy one.

Table 5.1 provides an overview of the elements behind a positive attitude towards doing the act – and thus whether the stakeholder is positive about contributing, and what you can work with.

The section above shows that it is not only important to know what the stakeholder believes doing an act entails. It is also important to know whether the stakeholder values the consequence or not, and whether the stakeholder finds it positive or burdensome, i.e. associated with a large cost, to perform the act that contributing requires.

*Table 5.1* What you can influence in the attitude towards doing the act

| *The stakeholder's …* | | *What it means* | *What you can work with* |
|---|---|---|---|
| Necessary contributions | | One or more acts that the project needs | Do not ask for more than necessary |
| Consequences | Costs | What it takes to perform the act | Facilitate doing the act so that it, for example, takes little time to do it |
| | Benefits | What the stakeholder gets out of doing the act | Think about compensating the stakeholder financially or otherwise, e.g. by influence on the project |
| Expectations | | The stakeholder's expectation of the needed contributions and the consequences of doing it | Be clear on what contributing requires from the stakeholder and what the consequences will be |
| Preferences | | The stakeholder's perception of whether the consequence of the act is valuable | Be sure to offer benefits that the stakeholder values and avoid costs that the stakeholder dislikes<br>Make the stakeholder aware of the value of the benefits that you offer and why the costs can be considered reasonable |

Furthermore, projects are often complex, consisting of many interconnected acts. Therefore, it is difficult for the stakeholder to assess the value of each individual act and thus also to understand the consequences of contributing. You must be aware of this and consider that the stakeholder may have completely different ideas and expectations of cost and benefits than you. This is a key to successful stakeholder engagement.

## The social norm

The second aspect behind the theory of planned behaviour is the social norm (Ajzen, 1985). Individuals supplement the logic of consequence with a *logic of appropriateness* (March & Olsen, 1996). This means that they consider what others see as *appropriate behaviour*. They ask themselves: what do others expect a person like me to do in this situation? Through interactions with the environment, stakeholders have developed an idea of how others see them; they have developed a *social identity*. In a project context, social identity is, among other things, linked to the role that the stakeholder has in the organization or in relation to the project. The stakeholder will try to behave in a way that the stakeholder believes supports his or her social identity. For example, a manager may feel that he should accept being a project owner, even though he is not interested in being one, because he believes that this is expected in his job.

Persons who, in a project context, can influence the stakeholder via the social norm, can be colleagues, the stakeholder's manager, or stakeholders whose interests the stakeholder represents, for example end users who influence a customer's requirements for materials to be used. The stakeholder may also consider the opinion of the project manager, especially if there is a professional or a personal relationship beforehand.

The influence of the social norm is *direct* and *conscious* when someone tells the stakeholder what they think is correct behaviour. The influence is *indirect*, when the stakeholder thinks about what others find he or she should do. It can also be *unconscious*, e.g. through influence from the organizational culture. It is a challenge for you, and possibly also for the stakeholder, that the influence from the social norm is often unconscious or at least not verbalized. This means that stakeholders cannot express how they are influenced and translate this into a reasoned attitude towards doing the act needed to contribute to the project.

## Perception of fairness

When stakeholders decide whether to contribute, they also assess whether they find that the project treats them and other stakeholders fairly. There are three dimensions to fairness (Bosse et al., 2009): (1) Is the *distribution* of benefits, side effects, and costs fair? In other words: do all stakeholders, including those with less or no power, receive a fair amount of value? (2) Are the *procedures* for stakeholder engagement fair? In other words: are stakeholders engaged in a transparent and fair way, e.g. in decision-making processes? (3) Is the *interaction* fair? In other words: do you and your team speak and behave politely and respectfully? And do you share information properly?

A typical example of perceived unfair treatment is how information is shared when changes are made to the project. If some stakeholders feel that they have been informed later than others, they may react strongly. The same applies if they have not received the information they need to make decisions. This can be due to distributional as well as procedural perceived lack of fairness. If the stakeholders in continuation of the episode cannot get an explanation for the unfair treatment, interactional unfairness is also at play.

The concept of perceived fairness (Bosse et al., 2009) implies that *stakeholders will be willing to lower their attempts to fulfil their self-interest if they find that there is fairness on all three dimensions.* That is, a stakeholder will be less focused on getting the most out of contributing if the stakeholder deems that there is distributional, procedural, and interactional fairness. On the other hand, *the stakeholders will focus on the fulfilment of their own needs and requirements if they have the impression that the project manager acts unfairly on any of the three dimensions.* This also applies if others are treated unfairly in the stakeholder's opinion.

Box 5.1 shows the dimensions that stakeholders assess in their perception of fairness.

**Box 5.1 Dimensions in the stakeholder's perception of fairness**

- Distribution of benefits, side effects, and costs
- Procedures
- Interactions

Source: Based on Bosse et al. (2009)

Stakeholders' perception of fairness is central. As a committed project manager or team member, you can easily see the project as the most important thing in the world and therefore justify all your decisions and actions with the project in mind. You may forget to see the project from the various stakeholders' perspectives. This can also include that you focus on having a good relationship with the individual stakeholder – and forget that the stakeholders may have *mutual relationships* and *interact* with each other. Typically, some of the stakeholders already know each other, and if not, at least some of them will come to know each other during the project. When they know each other, they are likely to share information about and attitudes towards the project and your management, including how you engage them. This can have a major impact on the stakeholders' perception of fairness. Benefits given to one stakeholder can easily become visible to other stakeholders, and it can therefore lead to feelings of unfair treatment if some stakeholders feel that you give larger benefits to some stakeholders than to others.

*Relationships are reciprocal*, and experiences in one interaction influence future interactions (Bosse et al., 2009). *Reciprocity* is an *ongoing process*, which includes many interactions in different situations before, during, and after the individual project. If a stakeholder gets more than expected in an interaction, this person will be willing to contribute more than what is strictly necessary at a later occasion. In this way, a collaboration can develop into an ongoing "gift exchange" (*positive reciprocity*), in which both parties reward each other in a positive, upward spiral (Akerlof, 1982). For example, a stakeholder may, during a pilot project to introduce new processes, offer to share his or her experiences at an information event that will be held in connection with the rollout of the new processes. This may result in the project manager involving the stakeholder more in decision-making about the project than originally planned. This may lead to greater commitment from the stakeholder, etc.

Unfortunately, collaboration can also develop into a negative, downward spiral, where the parties exchange *negative reciprocity* and give less and less to each other, or even start *sanctioning* each other (Bosse et al., 2009). If a stakeholder feels a deficiency in fairness on one or more of the three dimensions (distributional, procedural, and interactional fairness), he or she may choose to contribute less than the project needs or require larger benefits for contributing. Instead of "giving a gift", the person may "require payment" because of the perceived lack of fairness. You may then be disappointed because the stakeholder delivers less than you expected. This may result in you sanctioning the stakeholder by giving less in return in the next interaction, e.g. by withholding information. This creates a negative, downward spiral.

Be aware that individuals who feel that they have been treated unfairly will sanction the other party more severely than they will reward the person for a fair treatment (Offerman, 2002). This means that a great deal of effort is required to repair damage in the relationship with a stakeholder who has felt unfair treatment. It is thus very important not to disappoint the stakeholders. You can protect yourself against this by emphasizing alignment of expectations so that the stakeholders' expectations for attention and value creation from the project are realistic. An expression says it clearly: under-promise and overdeliver!

The need not to disappoint others can, for example, apply to your project owner. It is unfortunate if your project owner hears news about major challenges in the project from people other than yourself. Major news that the project owner hears from others can create uncertainty about whether there are other significant matters that you have not informed them about. Therefore, make sure that your project owner is well informed about the project. To give your project owner the opportunity to react to and digest big news about the project in peace and quiet, it is also important to be careful not to deliver big news while others are present. This may be perceived as unfair by the project owner.

The effects of our actions *accumulate over time*. Therefore, you should be aware that maximizing the project's benefits in the short term at the expense of fairness to stakeholders can have negative effects in the long run. You should also consider the formal and, not least, informal channels of influence between the project stakeholders and their stakeholders, because they may prove important for the stakeholder's decision to contribute or not. As part of this, you should consider what stakeholders value when judging what is fair in terms of reciprocity in relationships over time, and how others are rewarded for contributing. All of this will help predict how each stakeholder can be expected to act. This knowledge can also be used to create social pressure to contribute.

## Perceived ability to do the act

The stakeholder's *perceived ability to do the act* to contribute to the project can strengthen or weaken the intention to do so. This is the third aspect behind the intention to act.

Perceived ability to do the act concerns two issues. The first is the stakeholder's perception of *his or her qualifications* to do the act. Perhaps a stakeholder feels that she lacks the necessary skills to do the task needed, or that she cannot do the task in the allotted time.

The second issue is *whether the stakeholder is free to decide to carry out the action*. Maybe the stakeholder does not have a slot in her calendar at the allotted time or needs approval from a manager before doing the act. This issue is particularly relevant if the organizational culture focuses on formal hierarchy and procedures (Eskerod, 1997). In this type of organization, the stakeholder will tend to strictly adhere to contributing to the extent described in the formal agreement. This means that the stakeholder sees a contribution that is not stated in the contract as outside their capabilities.

Because the perceived ability to do the required act influences the intention to contribute, it is crucial that you consider whether the stakeholder will see themselves as able to do so. You should also consider whether it is up to the stakeholder to make the decision to do the act.

You can support contribution by increasing the stakeholder's knowledge and skills, e.g. through education and training. If you believe that the stakeholder has the necessary skills, you can seek to influence the stakeholder's perception of what the stakeholder can do. You can do this by providing precise information about the effort required and the tasks to be solved. Finally, you should consider whether you need to collaborate with one or more of the stakeholder's stakeholders, e.g. a superior who decides how the stakeholder uses his or her resources. Box 5.2 summarizes the elements of the perceived ability to do the act.

**Box 5.2 Elements of the perceived ability to do the act**

- Perceived qualifications in relation to what is required
- Perceived potential barriers such as lack of time, lack of tools, or lack of financial means
- Perceived lack of competence to decide to do the act

## Intention to contribute

The intention to contribute is based the stakeholder's expected positive consequences from contributing, influence from the social norm, perceived fairness, and the stakeholder's perceived ability to do the act. Table 5.2 builds on the wind turbine project from Chapter 4 and shows the elements that underlie the intention to contribute at a general level for the same three stakeholders. You will find an empty table in Appendix A. The result of the analysis will go into the stakeholder register.

## From intention to action

Intentions are not the same as actual behaviour (Ajzen, 1985). Some intentions never become actions, and actions are only partially carried out as planned. Something may happen that *prevents the act being done* or that in the end makes the act *irrelevant.* It may also be that the stakeholder is *not quite as good at doing the act* as expected, and this may influence the actual consequence of doing the act. A stakeholder who intends to go to a meeting may end up not attending because the their child becomes ill and they must stay home. It may also be that the stakeholder goes to the meeting but does not get to say anything, even though the plan was to speak. Finally, it may be that the stakeholder had planned a long, clear speech, but ends up saying something short and perhaps unclear.

Intentions may also not turn into action because they have *weakened over time.* This can happen if the intentions were not maintained and there has been a time lapse between forming the intention and carrying out the act. Therefore, it is important to continually work to ensure that the stakeholder has a strong intention to do the act required to contribute. This is especially true if obstacles may arise, or

*Table 5.2* Aspects behind the stakeholder's intention to contribute

| *Stakeholder* | *Expected consequences of contributing* | *Influences from social norm and perception of fairness* | *Perceived ability to do the act* | *Intention to contribute* |
|---|---|---|---|---|
| Customer X | A wind farm that works as agreed | Nothing in particular | Is concerned about whether they can specify the need sufficiently and precisely | Positive – will gain from the project |
| Head of development department | Relevant work for the department's employees | The work is in line with the department's expertise | Is worried about whether a specific, important bottleneck employee can contribute | Positive – it is part of the department head's obligations |
| Birder | Bird life is harmed | Other birders are very upset | The birding association can support a possible protest | Negative – will not refrain from protesting |

if the time lapse between forming the intention and doing the act is long. The intention can become so weak that the stakeholder forgets about it. You can avoid this by linking the intention to the time, and preferably also the place, of the actual act, so that the stakeholder visualizes their contributions and thus sees themselves contributing. This makes the leap to contributing easier.

## Consider the stakeholder's motivation to contribute

In this chapter, we have discussed the most important factors behind a stakeholder's intention to do the act(s) required to contribute to a project and how such an intention turns into action, i.e. a contribution. The expectations that the stakeholders have about possible benefits and costs associated with contributing to the project in the way you would like them to have a great impact on their attitude towards contributing. You must also bear in mind that stakeholders are influenced by what they think others think about them contributing or not, when they decide whether to contribute, as well as their perception of fairness in the project. Furthermore, they consider whether they have the skills and the opportunity to contribute as desired. You can help the stakeholder to contribute by helping the stakeholder make sense of contributing and by easing the act for the stakeholder. Also, remember that it may be necessary to remind the stakeholder to do the act if a long time passes between the intention to do so and the time when the project needs the contribution.

### Mini-case 5 Volunteering for the restoration of the Notre Dame Cathedral in Paris

On Monday, 15 April 2019 in the early evening, a fire broke out in the roof space of the iconic historical landmark, Notre Dame Cathedral, in Paris. With more than 400 firefighters engaged the fire was extinguished, but the roof, spire, and medieval framework were severely damaged.

Already the same night, the French president announced that the cathedral would be rebuilt. Hereafter a restoration project was established, a campaign to raise international funding initiated, and the duration of the project set to five years.

The project to rebuild the cathedral was supported from all over the world. An international non-profit group, *Carpenters Without Borders*, was invited to supply carpenters to apply woodworking techniques from former times to restore the cathedral in a way that was loyal to the original techniques.

Carpenters Without Borders is an association that undertakes workshops, where persons who are skilled and passionate about the woodworking trades work together to contribute to restoration projects, especially on historic monuments. The participants can be professionals, apprentices, and amateurs. Carpenters Without Borders has had workshop gatherings across the world, e.g. China, France, Romania, and the USA, for more than 40 years. For each workshop, the composition of the team is set up to match the needs for specific techniques.

Carpenters Without Borders formed a team of 25 professional carpenters to reconstruct one of the gothic trusses of Notre Dame. They would cut the old truss down and manually replace it with a new one made from 20 carefully selected oak trees.

The workshop was carried out with great success. It contributed well to the restoration project. Notre Dame Cathedral reopened on 7 December 2024, which was five and a half years after the fire.

Sources: Carpenters Without Borders (n.d.), Hinnant (2019), and Picard (2023)

*The case illustrates that a project may need very specific contributions, e.g. application of skills, from stakeholders who are scattered across the world. To restore Notre Dame Cathedral as close as possible to the original format, the project organization needed carpenters who were able and willing to apply ancient construction techniques.*

*We can look into some of the thoughts that the team members from Carpenters Without Borders might have had when contemplating if they would participate in the reconstruction through the lens of the theory of planned behaviour.*

*Considering the consequences of doing the act – participating in the reconstruction work – a volunteer carpenter would think about the benefits and the costs involved in participating. Possible benefits could include the joy of using the learned ancient techniques, pride in contributing to the restoration, and togetherness with the other volunteers.*

*Considering the social norm – what others think about the participation – the carpenter might think about the family, the personal network, and a possible employer. It will support signing up for participation, if these persons all are expected to be positive. It can weaken the intention to contribute, if any of them are negative.*

*Considering the perceived ability to do the act – if the carpenter possesses the right skills and can decide whether to participate – the carpenter may think about his or her level of skills in working with the specific techniques needed as compared to other carpenters, if he or she has time available and the financial means to go to Paris. Furthermore, the carpenter will wonder if their employer allows participation and if they will be selected for participation by the association.*

## References

Ajzen, I. (1985). From intentions to actions: A theory of planned behavior. In J. Kuhl & J. Beckmann (Eds.), *Action-control: From cognition to behavior* (pp. 11–39). Springer.

Akerlof, G. A. (1982). Labor contracts as a partial gift exchange. *Quarterly Journal of Economics*, 97 (4), 543–569.

Bosse, D. A., Phillips, R. A., & Harrison, J. S. (2009). Stakeholders, reciprocity, and firm performance. *Strategic Management Journal*, 30 (4), 447–456.

Carpenters Without Borders (n.d.). *Manifesto for Carpenters Without Borders.* https://www.charpentiers-sans-frontieres.com/. Accessed 10 August 2025.

Eskerod, P. (1997). *Nye perspektiver på fordeling af menneskelige ressourcer i et projektorganiseret multiprojekt-miljø* [New perspectives on the allocation of human resources in a project-organized multi-project environment]. PhD thesis. Handelshøjskole Syd.

Hinnant, L. (2019). 66 minutes: The frantic race to save Notre Dame. *AP News.* Web article published 17 April. https://apnews.com/article/fires-ap-top-news-paris-international-news-europe-e9cc2e0e2ce84b7a82abbc23e50bcea1. Accessed 10 August 2025.

March, J. G. (1994). *Primer on decision making: How decisions happen.* The Free Press.

March, J. G., & Olsen, J. P. (1996). Institutional perspectives on political institutions. *Governance*, 9 (3), 247–264.

Offerman, T. (2002). Hurting hurts more than helping helps. *European Economic Review*, 46 (8), 1423–1437.

Picard, K. (2023). *A Lincoln carpenter landed a plumb position rebuilding Notre-Dame Cathedral in Paris.* Web article published 12 July. https://www.sevendaysvt.com/arts-culture/a-lincoln-carpenter-landed-a-plumb-position-rebuilding-notre-dame-cathedral-in-paris-38642526. Accessed 10 August 2025.

Simon, H. A. (1956). Rational choice and the structure of the environment. *Psychological Review*, 63 (2), 129–138.

Smith, A. (1776). *Wealth of nations: An inquiry into the nature and causes of the wealth of nations: A selected edition* (2008 ed.). Oxford Paperbacks.

# 6 Which stakeholders should you prioritize?

You don't have unlimited resources available for your stakeholder engagement, and you can therefore only give limited attention to each stakeholder. This means that you need to prioritize your efforts among the stakeholders. For this purpose, you need an overview of your stakeholders and their needs for your attention. This chapter presents ways to achieve this, among other things by creating a stakeholder register.

## Overview and prioritization

The stakeholder's potential to influence the project plays a significant role in the prioritization of your efforts along with the stakeholder's attitude towards contributing. Figure 4.1 showed how stakeholders can be placed in one of four categories based on their potential to influence the project positively and negatively. This categorization can be used to prepare a *stakeholder potential map*. You can place all stakeholders in the map, or just one type of stakeholder, e.g. the key players. The purpose is to assess the stakeholders' *relative potential to influence* the project positively or negatively and to get an overview of the number of stakeholders in each category.

Stakeholders are represented by bubbles. You can refine the map by drawing the stakeholder bubbles in different sizes depending on the size of the group behind each stakeholder label, e.g. customers. You can also use colours to highlight the type of stakeholder – customers in one colour and suppliers in another. The stakeholders' potential to influence the project positively or negatively varies across issues. Therefore, you should ideally create a map for each issue that you are

DOI: 10.4324/9781003712695-6

working on, so that you can focus the stakeholders' potential to influence the specific issue at hand.

Figure 6.1 shows an example of a stakeholder potential map. The project owner and the customer are both *key players*, while the ministry is a *showstopper*. The supplier is *resourceful*, and the communications department employee is a *marginal* stakeholder. So is the birder. It is difficult to classify the head of the development department.

The stakeholder potential map shows, as the name suggests, the *potential* of the stakeholders to positively or negatively influence the project. The map does not indicate whether you can expect them to realize this potential, i.e. whether they will act to positively or negatively influence the project. To assess this, you need to add whether the stakeholder *expects to be influenced* by the project in a positive or negative way.

Whether you should work actively with a group of stakeholders depends on how much you need to move the stakeholder from one category to another. For example, you must address if a key player has a negative attitude towards contributing as necessary, while you can spend fewer resources on active stakeholder engagement with a positive marginal stakeholder. On the other hand, it may be appropriate to spend time on a marginal stakeholder if this stakeholder is particularly negatively influenced by the project.

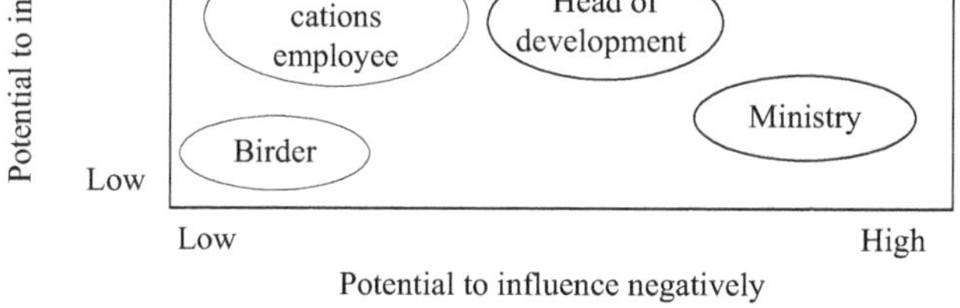


*Figure 6.1* A stakeholder potential map
Source: Inspired by Savage et al. (1991)

To see which stakeholders you need to work with, you can create a stakeholder commitment matrix (McElroy & Mills, 2003). The matrix contains a row for each stakeholder and five columns for each stakeholder's possible commitment, which are: *active opposition, passive opposition, neutral, passive support*, and *active support*. For each stakeholder, mark the current commitment with an X in the relevant category, and another sign, e.g. an O, in the category the project needs the stakeholder to be in. Arrows show which way and how far the stakeholder must move to change attitude from X to O.

Figure 6.2 shows an example of a stakeholder commitment matrix. The suppliers are neutral, and that is what the project manager wants them to be. Top management supports the project, but the project manager needs the support to be more active, e.g. in the form of an inspiring speech given by the top manager or a statement from the manager in a relevant medium. Finally, the colleagues in the base organization are against the project, but without acting on it (i.e. they are passively against). That may be sufficient. But it means that they probably will not lend a helping hand if needed. Therefore, the project manager would like them to change their commitment so that they are more positive towards the project; preferably to active support, but maybe passive support is enough, so that, for example, they don't speak against colleagues supporting the project.

The project manager typically wants to move stakeholders in the right direction in the table, i.e. towards being more positive about the project or contributing. However, it may also be necessary to move stakeholders towards the left in the table. This is usually because the

| Stakeholder | Active opposition | Passive opposition | Neutral | Passive support | Active support |
|---|---|---|---|---|---|
| Supplier | | | XO | | |
| Top management | | | | X→ | →→O |
| Colleagues in the base organization | | X → | →→→ | →→ O | |
| Chief Financial Officer | | | | O ←← | ←← X |

X=current position, O=required/desired position,
←=direction, desired movement of the stakeholder

*Figure 6.2* Stakeholder commitment matrix with example
Source: Based on McElroy & Mills (2003)

project manager wants a stakeholder to be less active in their support and perhaps even stop being interested in the project (see Figure 6.2). Perhaps a positive stakeholder interferes in favour of the project, thereby creating unnecessary noise about it. For example, a CFO may actively support a change project aimed at better working conditions, focusing on the possible cost savings that the project will result in. This does not help the project. It could also be a department manager who is very interested in a project and therefore constantly makes suggestions that the project manager cannot accommodate and thus needs to find arguments to refuse.

The stakeholder commitment matrix provides a good overview of the stakeholders' need for attention. It highlights the stakeholders that need attention because the project needs them to change or strengthen their commitment (moving from active to passive or the other way around). It also shows that some stakeholders are not in need of attention at present because their commitment towards the project or towards contributing is already as necessary. For example, it is not necessary for all stakeholders to actively support the project. In many cases, it is enough if a negative stakeholder refrains from acting on their attitude. If they appear to be in passive rather than active opposition, there is no need to give this stakeholder much attention.

The need to spend effort on the stakeholder – which we call the stakeholder's *need for attention* – is determined by three aspects: (1) the stakeholder's positive or negative influence from the project (the larger the influence, especially negative, the more the stakeholder can be expected to act on the influence); (2) the stakeholder's potential to influence the project positively; and (3) the stakeholder's potential to influence the project negatively. Table 6.1 shows the eight possible stakeholder categories created by the three dimensions of influence, and the labels we have given them, as well as their need for attention.

We have used *different shades of grey* as a simple way to show which stakeholders need attention and whom you should therefore prioritize for active engagement. Dark grey indicates that the stakeholder is in high need of attention, light grey indicates that the stakeholder is in some need for attention, and white indicates that the stakeholder is in no need for attention right now. It is important to note that you cannot simply ignore "white" stakeholders. You need to monitor them to see if they move to one of the other categories.

*Table 6.1* Stakeholder categories and their need for attention

| *Perceived influence from the project* | *Potential to influence the project positively* | *Potential to influence the project negatively* | *Category and need for attention* |
|---|---|---|---|
| Positive | ✓ | ✓ | Positive key player |
| Negative | ✓ | ✓ | Negative key player |
| Positive | ✓ | | Positive resourceful |
| Negative | ✓ | | Negative resourceful |
| Positive | | ✓ | Positive showstopper |
| Negative | | ✓ | Negative showstopper |
| Positive | | | Positive marginal |
| Negative | | | Negative marginal |

Notes: Dark grey=high need for attention, light grey=some need for attention, white=no need for attention now

The categorization of the individual stakeholder depends on the *issue at hand*. For example, a line manager is a key player because of control over important resources in the form of relevant employees in connection with the issue of composition of the project team. The same line manager is a marginal stakeholder when it comes to issues such as the selection of the project's subcontractors or the decision on the project's scope.

The categorization also depends on the *project management phase*. In the implementation phase, one out of several end users who are willing to test the product might be categorized as a resourceful stakeholder (the potential to influence negatively is low, as there are alternative users), while a test expert who is difficult to replace would be a key player. In other phases, both stakeholders are marginal. Another example is a resourceful stakeholder, e.g. a consultant, who may become a key player as the project progresses. This happens if the interdependence between the project and the stakeholder grows, making it more expensive and more difficult to replace the consultant, augmenting the stakeholder's potential to harm the project by, for example, leaving it.

To prioritize your effort towards stakeholders, you must assess their direct or indirect ability to influence the project positively and negatively as well as the stakeholder's expected intention to do so. When doing so, remember that the stakeholder may be involved in networks with other stakeholders, and that a stakeholder without the ability to influence the project may need attention because the project influences the stakeholder negatively.

## The stakeholder register

In this and the two previous chapters, we have presented the stakeholder analysis. It leads to a filled-out stakeholder register like the one displayed in Table 6.2. The register contains a row for each stakeholder, and the information in the register is a combination of Tables 4.1, 4.2, 5.2, and 6.1, supplemented by consideration of challenges and opportunities in working with the stakeholder, e.g. with input from Figure 4.2. You will find an empty register in Appendix B. The register must be completed as follows:

1. Stakeholder. Who are the individuals or entities that can influence or be influenced by the project? Write either role or name (or both).
2. Possible influence. How and to what extent can the stakeholder influence or be influenced by the project, and is it positive or negative? (Table 4.1)
3. Necessary contributions. How does the project need the stakeholder to contribute? What should the stakeholder do or not do? (Table 4.2)
4. Requirements and wishes. What does the stakeholder require or want in return for the needed contributions?
5. Intention to contribute. Is the stakeholder positive or negative towards doing the act to contribute as needed? Use the elements behind the intention to act to contribute to assess this. (Table 5.2)
6. Challenges and opportunities. Are the stakeholder's requirements urgent and/or legitimate? What can strengthen the intention to contribute? Can an intention to contribute be put under pressure or supported? Can the stakeholder form networks with other stakeholders? (Figure 4.2)
7. Category and need for attention. Choose from the categories in Table 6.1 and use different shades of grey to mark the need for attention.

To support your understanding, we have filled in the stakeholder register in Table 6.2 with three of the stakeholders from a change

*Table 6.2* Stakeholder register with example

| *Stakeholder* | *Possible influence* | *Necessary contributions* | *Requirements and wishes* | *Intention to contribute* | *Challenges and opportunities* | *Category and need for attention* |
|---|---|---|---|---|---|---|
| Project owner | Sets the frames and resources for the project | Continue support | Project completed within time and budget<br>Project brings the planned value | Has been involved in proposing the project | May lose interest as the project progresses | Positive key player |
| Union representative | Can pass on information and can influence employees | Loyally provide information from and to employees<br>Play along positively | To be able to help ensure that the project does not have any or a few negative side effects for the members | Can see both positive and negative consequences | Can be challenged by negative employees | Key player (neither positive nor negative) |
| Negative employees | Can be difficult to motivate to participate in testing | Work loyally to complete tasks in the new way during the testing phase | To be sure that the project will have no or few negative side effects for them | Are worried about whether they can perform the new tasks and whether their qualifications are no longer sufficient<br>Are also concerned about the time spent | Can team up with other negative members | Negative marginal – but as group key player |

Notes: Dark grey=high need for attention, light grey=some need for attention, white=no need for attention now project that is to introduce a new way of working to streamline some workflows. They are the project owner, the union representative, and a group of negative employees. There are of course more stakeholders, including employees who are positive about the change.

As an example, we will take a closer look at the union representative. This person can influence the project to some extent by providing or withholding information to the members of the union and possibly mobilize them to resistance. The project manager needs the union representative to contribute by loyally sharing information to and from the employees. The project manager also wishes the union representative to be positive about the change, but this is not strictly necessary. The union representative has a mixed intention towards contributing as the project manager needs. This is mostly based on unclear consequences of the project. In continuation of this, the union representative expects that a positive contribution will be rewarded with influence on the project, so that she can help ensure that there are as few negative side effects as possible for the union members. The project manager is concerned that the union representative may swing to a more negative attitude towards supporting the project due to pressure from negative members (the social norm). The conclusion is that the union representative is currently a key player (neither positive nor negative) who needs some attention.

The stakeholder register contains your assessment of the stakeholders. You may occasionally make some quick remarks in it that may be perceived differently depending on the eyes that see. Therefore, keep the register in a locked place and consider who you share it with.

## Overview of tools

Box 6.1 provides a comprehensive overview of the stakeholder analysis tools that we have presented in this and the previous chapters.

### Box 6.1 Overview of tools for stakeholder analysis

For an overview of the stakeholders:

- The stakeholder register with information about each stakeholder, necessary contributions and requirements and wishes (Table 6.2 from Tables 4.1, 4.2, 5.2 and 6.1)

For categorizing each stakeholder and the need to prioritize them:

- The stakeholders and their potential for influence (Table 4.1)
- The necessary involvement of the stakeholders (Table 4.2)
- Stakeholder potential categorization – influence positively or negatively (Figure 4.1)
- Stakeholder network – interest and power base (Figure 4.2)
- The elements that you can work with in the attitude towards doing the act to contribute (Table 5.1)
- Elements of the stakeholders' intention to participate (Table 5.2)

To assess the need for prioritization in relative terms – all stakeholders in the same figure:

- Stakeholder potential map (Figure 6.1) – analogous to Figure 4.1

To assess the need to collaborate with the stakeholder:

- The stakeholder register – categorization of the stakeholder in relation to power to influence positively or negatively and how the stakeholder is influenced – strength and direction (Table 6.2)

## The stakeholder register is dynamic

The stakeholder register can take on other forms than the register we have presented here. It can be a stack of Post-its with the names of the stakeholders, a list of their names and contact information, or an advanced database with detailed and structured information about each stakeholder. Several factors influence which type is most appropriate: the size and complexity of the project, the number of individuals involved in the stakeholder engagement, the culture of the base organization, and the administrative resources available.

The more complex the project, the more structure and clarity is needed, because the information will then have to be shared by more individuals. Remember that maintaining a detailed stakeholder register requires data discipline and resources. Therefore, it may be a good decision to go with a relatively simple solution.

Regardless of the form, the stakeholder register is not set in stone. First and foremost, a complete identification of the stakeholders may not be possible at the beginning of the project, as this requires knowledge that is unavailable at this point. Furthermore, projects are dynamic. Plans, and possibly scope and even purpose can change. At the same time, new stakeholders may appear while other stakeholders may leave the project or become less important along the way.

This means that you need to do several stakeholder analyses during the project. We suggest that you review your stakeholder register at important gates in the project and update it accordingly.

**Mini-case 6 The project's stakeholders on social media**

Western Sydney International Airport is a construction project in Australia. The Australian government has promised to inform the population about the project to establish the airport on an ongoing basis. The project uses the social media platforms Facebook, Instagram, LinkedIn, X, and YouTube to this end.

The communication on social media is about the airport itself as well as the changes for the local community and other stakeholders that the establishment of the airport entails. The project communicates, among other things, about an experience centre (which interested parties can visit to gain knowledge about the new airport), information meetings, the airport's importance for local employment, the naming of the airport, future flight routes (including noise pollution), and the valuation of land in the vicinity of the airport.

The project's accounts on Facebook and LinkedIn have the most followers. The project mostly communicates with its stakeholders on Facebook. The project does so by posting about the above topics, sometimes with videos or photos. Stakeholders interact by liking, using different emojis, commenting, and sharing.

A research project on the airport's use of social media found that 391 different stakeholders (represented by user ID) had commented on the project's post about the experience centre at the time of the data collection. Of the 391 stakeholders, 302 commented only once, while 58 stakeholders commented twice. Only five stakeholders commented seven or more times. The most active stakeholder commented 34 times on posts about the experience centre.

The comments from stakeholders were mostly short and positive comments, e.g. in the form of questions about the experience centre's opening hours. Only a few people reacted with negative comments. In most cases, the project failed to respond to these negative comments, but surprisingly, in some cases, another Facebook user stepped in and reprimanded a critical stakeholder with correct information or defended the project.

There are some examples of the project responding directly to comments from stakeholders. In these cases, the stakeholder entered a short dialogue reflecting the stakeholder's knowledge of and interest in the project.

It was not possible to analyse which stakeholders the project should prioritize because so few (in relative terms) commented more than once or twice.

Sources: Chung et al. (2023) and Jepsen et al. (2025)

*The case is an example of how a project can use social media, not least for the local area, giving information during the project's implementation phase.*

*The case reminds us that social media can help stakeholders activate their potential to influence the project negatively and positively. It also reminds us that the communication is open to both the project and to other stakeholders, and that anyone who has an interest in the project can communicate, to reach stakeholders. Therefore, it is important that the project prioritizes to respond to stakeholders who communicate with the project via these media. You should do so properly and honestly.*

*The case also illustrates that it is difficult, if not impossible, to assess individual stakeholders with data from their behaviour on social media in quite the same way as we recommend in this chapter. The thing is that social media provides little information about stakeholders and their opinions. Some stakeholders may be invisible, as they do not post or comment but only follow the communication. Others only make themselves known with comments or other activity once or a few times. The fact that stakeholders are active or not cannot be used as an indicator of their interest in and knowledge of the project, because they may not like to be visible on social media, or they use other media to communicate with or follow the project.*

*However, the project can use the communication on social media to find issues that interest several stakeholders, e.g. noise from overflights. The project can use this information to prioritize communicating about these issues, thereby taking take care of many of the questions and concerns that the stakeholders have.*

## References

Chung, K. S. K., Eskerod, P., Jepsen, A. L., & Zhang, J. (2023). Response strategies for community stakeholder engagement on social media: A case study of a large infrastructure project. *International Journal of Project Management*, 41 (5), 102495.

Jepsen, A. L., Eskerod, P., Chung, K. S. K., Zhang, J., & Ortiz, M. (2025). Using websites and social media to support local community stakeholder attendance at project town hall meetings. *Project Leadership & Society*, 6, 100164.

McElroy, B., & Mills, C. (2003). Managing stakeholders. In R. J. Turner (Ed.), *People in project management* (pp. 99–118). Gower.

Savage, G.T., Nix, T. W., Whitehead, C. J., & Blair, J. D. (1991). Strategies for assessing and managing organizational stakeholders. *Academy of Management Perspectives*, 5 (2), 61–75.

# 7 Sources of information about stakeholders

Stakeholder analysis requires that you know a great deal about the stakeholders. You need to know their resources so that you can assess their potential to influence the project positively or negatively. You also need to understand how they perceive the project and their influence on it, and how they think the project might influence them. This will help you assess their intention to contribute to the project. How to obtain the information is the subject of this chapter.

## Data sources

There are different ways of acquiring knowledge about stakeholders, and you must decide which you will pursue to acquire the knowledge you need. One way is to base your knowledge on colleting *primary data*. This is fresh data that you collect for your specific project. You can also base your knowledge on *secondary data*. This is data that has already been collected for other purposes. Finally, you can base your knowledge on *generalizations* from similar situations (also called assumptions). Table 7.1 summarizes the three types of data and their advantages and disadvantages. We will talk more about them below.

You can collect *primary data* by interacting with stakeholders through various types of interviews or questionnaires. You can also observe stakeholders and infer their thinking from their behaviour. If you do so, you should engage in dialogue with the stakeholders to verify the perception you have gained through observation. Primary data can be collected in a *structured way* via questionnaires, in workshops, or through more or less structured qualitative personal or group interviews. Primary data can also be collected in an

DOI: 10.4324/9781003712695-7

*Table 7.1* Advantages and disadvantages of different data types

| *Data type* | *Characteristics* | *Advantages* | *Disadvantages* |
|---|---|---|---|
| Primary | Collected for a specific purpose in your current project, e.g. an interview with a stakeholder | Fits the purpose exactly<br>An opportunity to interact with the stakeholders | Requires professional insight into research methodology to generate credible results<br>Is relatively expensive in time and effort for you and the stakeholders |
| Secondary | Collected for other purposes, such as accounting or statistical purposes | Relatively inexpensive<br>Often covers a wide range of areas, e.g. many persons over time | May not fit what you need to know<br>Often at an aggregate level<br>Usually doesn't cover how people think or feel |
| Generalizations | No concrete data<br>Just what you assume<br>Based on experiences with or knowledge about similar persons or situations | Cheap and fast | Can be very influenced by bias and that the assumptions may not match reality at all (see Table 7.2) |

*unstructured way* in meetings, informally at the coffee machine, or at social events. Structured data collection has the advantage that it is explicitly planned, which ensures that the required information is collected and that there is documentation for how the data were collected.

A *questionnaire*, possibly used in a survey, can be a good option if you need simple information about many stakeholders. Questionnaires have a fixed structure and provide mainly quantitative data. The structured data means that the data processing can be done using statistical software or in a spreadsheet. All respondents get the same questions, and this allows comparison across stakeholders. The *disadvantage* of the questionnaire as a data collection instrument is that the data collection is inflexible because the questions are fixed once the questionnaire has been distributed. This means that there is only limited opportunity for the individual stakeholder to add extra information to their answer, and you cannot include new topics that you may later find out are important.

If you need in-depth knowledge about your stakeholders, we recommend that you use *qualitative methods* such as semi- or unstructured interviews, or one of the various collaborative methods that can be facilitated in a workshop. It is of course important that you, by way of a preplanned structure, get information about the topics that you consider important for the project, but you should also allow space for stakeholders to raise topics that are important to them. Therefore, *semi-structured interviews*, using an interview guide, possibly in a workshop, are a good option. In a semi-structured interview, you define in advance the topics you want to cover, but you are flexible in terms of the order and new topics that arise along the way. You can conduct interviews or other interactions with stakeholders *individually* or *in a group*. The advantage of interviewing stakeholders individually is that the interview takes place in a private space, so it is confidential. The disadvantage is that it requires more resources than interviewing several stakeholders in a single session.

*Group interviews* can be conducted as a facilitated workshop or a focus group. In both interview formats, the interviewer plays a slightly different role than in traditional interviews. In a *facilitated workshop*, a facilitator asks the participants to carry out specific tasks, e.g. to try out a pilot version of the project's deliverables. In a *focus group*, a moderator asks participants to discuss a topic, e.g. their attitude towards contributing to the project and what they expect to get out of it. The facilitator's or the moderator's role is to steer the discussion. This means keeping it on track and ensuring that everyone is given the opportunity to express their opinions and come up with ideas. Facilitators and moderators should also aim to prevent peer pressure towards certain opinions. An *advantage* of group interviews is that the interaction between participants can make it easier for them to be open, because the situation is less formal than if each interviewee is alone with an interviewer. In this situation, it can happen that the interviewee waits for the interviewer to take the lead, or that the interviewee experiences the interview as an interrogation and therefore is too guarded to really provide personal information.

Collecting primary data via interaction with the stakeholder is costly, but it *can be very beneficial* to do so in the early stages of the project because it offers an opportunity for the stakeholder and the project to share information as well as increase the stakeholder's motivation to contribute (Jepsen & Eskerod, 2009). This is because the stakeholder may become more positive towards the project as the conversation with the project manager heightens insights about the project. At the same time, the stakeholder can contribute relevant insights and reveal concerns. Hopefully, the stakeholder will feel heard and included in the project – and even invited to co-create ideas and solutions. Interaction can also help to align expectations.

Unfortunately, interaction with the stakeholder to collect primary data is not without challenges. It can *create or increase the stakeholder's expectations* of influence on and value from the project. This can be risky, as you may not be able or willing to meet the expectations. Excessive expectations can be particularly challenging if you are interacting with stakeholders individually. If you spend a lot of resources uncovering the detailed wishes of each stakeholder, you may end up with many requirements and wishes that are incompatible. To prevent this from happening, you may benefit from creating a forum, e.g. a workshop, where you can interact with several stakeholders at the same time. This way, the stakeholders can get a sense of others' requirements and wishes, compare them to their own requirements and wishes, and get a realistic sense of what is possible in the project.

You can also use *secondary data* to gain knowledge about stakeholders. This is data that already exists because it has been produced for purposes other than the current stakeholder engagement. Relevant *data sources* are, for example, official documents such as project descriptions, contracts, role descriptions for the project organization, or minutes from project meetings. Databases with company or market information can also be relevant. Furthermore, professional content on social media such as LinkedIn or on stakeholders' websites, e.g. a customer's website, or the website of an interest group, may be useful. Personal social media like Facebook or Instagram may also be relevant. You should be aware that it is difficult to identify stakeholders via social media, because many refrain from posting or commenting, and only follow accounts passively. Researching on social media can therefore give a distorted picture of stakeholders (Chung et al., 2023). You can facilitate your search for knowledge about stakeholders and structure the data that you find by using AI (artificial intelligence). Research shows that AI has great potential to help you categorize your stakeholders accurately because AI can perform a more objective and complex analysis than the human brain can. For example, it is possible to group stakeholders based on a wide range of characteristics (Mariani et al., 2023).

Secondary data have the *advantage* that they can provide you with important information without the risk and time associated with collecting primary data. Furthermore, existing data are often more accurate than what the stakeholder can recall when they are interviewed or respond to a questionnaire. This is especially true if it concerns facts that are a little further back in time, such as what was agreed upon at the start of the project. It may be difficult to remember, but it is in the contract. Secondary data also have *limits*. They mostly describe facts, and not so much why or how the facts came about. The requirements – and perhaps only the most important requirements – are written into the documents, but not the discussions that lead to the requirements, and thus not the wishes and concerns of stakeholders.

A third way to create the necessary information base is to use various *generalizations* to imagine what the stakeholder will do and think, typically based on your *own experiences* with them. Maybe you have collaborated with the stakeholder before. Based on that, you form an expectation about factors that influence the stakeholder's perception of fairness in the project's information and decision-making processes. Generalizations can also be based on *personal characteristics* such as the stakeholder's role in the organization, professional background, or other markers.

It can be *risky to rely on generalizations* because, roughly speaking, they are imagination. You also fail to take advantage of your opportunities to engage stakeholders in the project through direct contact. This can have the side effect that stakeholders think it is strange that they are not involved at all: "they could have just asked me", they might say to each other when something goes wrong.

Table 7.2 shows two types of generalizations and, for inspiration, some questions you can ask yourself if you must base your understanding of the stakeholder on generalizations. As the table shows, you need to carefully consider what you are generalizing from, and whether you might need to spend resources on collecting primary or secondary data instead of generalizing.

*Table 7.2* Generalizations as a basis for knowledge

| *Generalization from* | *Assumption behind generalization* | *What to watch out for* | *Questions to ask* |
|---|---|---|---|
| Own experience | The stakeholder will behave in the same way in this project as before | Maybe this situation is different, or the stakeholder has changed | How was the stakeholder's involvement in similar projects? Is anything different this time? Does the stakeholder seem reliable, e.g. do the stakeholder's words and actions match? |
| Personal characteristics such as role or education | Individuals with certain characteristics are similar, so it is possible to generalize based on these characteristics | Individuals with the same educational background, etc. can be very different | What would a similar stakeholder do in a similar situation? |

## Techniques for facilitating workshops

In a facilitated workshop, participants must complete a task under guidance of a facilitator. There are several techniques for this purpose. We show a selection in Table 7.3, which we will comment on below.

The first technique is to let the stakeholder *reflect on experiences.* This is especially valuable when the issue is discussion and planning of the project process. For example, you can ask the stakeholders to reflect on the following:

- Mention three good and three bad experiences from similar projects
- What was particularly good or particularly bad about the communication process in the most recent project you participated in?

Discussion of personal good and bad experiences can help stakeholders clarify and express their requirements, wishes, concerns, and preferences. The discussion can make it easier to understand the

*Table 7.3* Some workshop techniques

| *Technique* | *Focus* | *Strengths* | *Weaknesses* |
| --- | --- | --- | --- |
| Reflection on experiences | The past – to learn about requirements, wishes, concerns and preferences relevant for the project | Stakeholders can formulate examples of what they like and dislike based on an explicit range of events | Stakeholders may have difficulty remembering specific events and causal relationships<br>Actions, in hindsight, appear more planned and well-considered than they were |
| Future scenarios | The future – to learn the stakeholders' expectations of the project outcome | It lets the stakeholder imagine and show or formulate how they see a future with the project's deliverables | It can be difficult for stakeholders to imagine and talk about the future – it's fantasy, after all |
| Systemic constellation | Stakeholders as part of a system – to learn about own perception of the stakeholders' mutual relationships | It enlightens the position of the stakeholder in relation to other stakeholders | It may seem too abstract<br>It may require a facilitator |
| MoSCoW prioritization technique | Prioritization of requirements and wishes | It clarifies which requirements are very important and raises awareness that some requirements may not actually be requirements | It can be difficult to separate requirements and wishes on four levels |
| Sorting techniques | Prioritization of requirements and wishes | Streamlines a process where many alternatives need to be compared | It can be difficult to formulate the right comparisons of requirements |

reason behind their intention to contribute or not. If the reflections take place in a workshop, stakeholders can inspire each other. At the same time, a workshop helps the stakeholders get to know each other. The weakness of this technique is that stakeholders may have difficulty remembering specific events and causal relationships – and perhaps, with hindsight, see their actions as more planned and well-considered than they were.

The *future scenario technique* attempts to clarify and perhaps influence the stakeholder's expectations for the future (Wack, 1985). This is done by asking the stakeholder to explain how she expects the project will generate value for her. Stakeholders can talk about their expectations for the future, or they can express how they see themselves in a future situation through role-playing or drawings. You can ask stakeholders to do this in different contexts. In a digital transformation project in a hospital, the stakeholder might be a nurse who is a representative of this staff group. To understand how the nurse sees himself using a new device, you can ask him to describe how he sees himself doing it.

A weakness of the future scenario technique is that it requires the stakeholder to be able to imagine the future. This can be difficult. You can therefore support the technique by describing the deliverables or perhaps showing prototypes of them. You can also describe the work processes in which the deliverables, e.g. an IT system or a new piece of equipment, will be used.

The method *systemic constellation* focuses on an individual's (unconscious) perception and inner picture of the stakeholders in relation to each other (Huemann et al., 2016). In the constellation, distance and direction of attention express their mutual relationship.

The individual conducting the constellation is called the constellation owner. It might be yourself as the project manager or someone from the team. The constellation owner maps out the stakeholders by using objects or humans to represent the stakeholders. The actual stakeholders should not participate in the constellation. The constellation owner can get help in creating the map and interpreting it from a *facilitator*.

The session starts with the facilitator having a dialogue with the constellation owner about the issue to be worked on. The dialogue clarifies which stakeholders are relevant to the issue. The constellation owner then chooses an object (or a person) to represent each stakeholder in the constellation and places the objects in relation to each other. Some should be close to each other, others far from each other. Some are facing each other because they have a collaboration or focus on each other in the project. Others look away from each other because they are unaware of each other or are focused on other stakeholders. Along the way, the facilitator can ask questions about the constellation to help the constellation owner reflect on the constellation as an image of the situation as she or he sees it.

This process continues until an initial setup – the current stakeholder constellation for the issue at hand – is reached. It is reached when the constellation owner intuitively senses that all the objects representing the stakeholders in the constellation are correctly positioned. The initial setup can be retained for later use, e.g. on a photo or a simple drawing of the constellation. The next step is that the constellation owner gains an understanding of the current situation by focusing on each stakeholder and their relationships with the rest of the system. When this is in place, the facilitator asks the constellation owner to move the objects representing the stakeholders to an ideal situation for the issue at hand. This can be done in several steps. The constellation owner again reflects on the constellation when the ideal situation is in place and thereby gains a better understanding of it.

The constellation process is followed by a debriefing session with those who have participated in the session. In this way, everyone can provide input to the constellation owner about the issue which the constellation owner wanted to reflect upon with the constellation. The constellation owner can then use the insights gained in his or her further project work. The constellation helps participants gain a deeper understanding of the stakeholders than traditional stakeholder analyses do, because it works with the participants' unconscious perceptions and assumptions about the relationships between them.

The *MoSCoW prioritization technique* is a well-known technique for getting stakeholders to prioritize their requirements and wishes. The technique was developed by Clegg and Barker (1994). The name MoSCoW comes from the words *Must have, Should have, Could have*, and *Won't have. Must have* means that the stakeholder will not contribute to the project or believe that the project is a success unless the requirement is met. *Should have* requirements should be met as far as possible. *Could have* should be met if doing so does not negatively influence other requirements and wishes. *Won't have* requirements cannot be met in this project. They are outside the project scope but may be relevant in a later project or a later version of the project's deliverables. When using the MoSCoW prioritization technique, you must first identify the stakeholders' requirements and wishes. Then, for each requirement and wish, ask each stakeholder to indicate whether it is required, should be met, possibly can be met, or is out of scope. The categorization can help both the project and stakeholders understand what is important to prioritize, if it is not possible to meet all the stakeholder's requirements and wishes during the project.

The final technique is *sorting*, which comprises several techniques. Sorting is suitable for uncovering and understanding stakeholders' priorities in situations where several different requirements cannot be met at once. For example, you may need to decide whether it is so important that the project delivers on time that deliverables can be changed to achieve it, if the project comes under time pressure; or whether it is so important that the deliverables are exactly as agreed that the stakeholder can accept the project being delayed. The former may be relevant if the project involves delivering a live show on New Year's Eve on TV, while the latter may be relevant if the project is to deliver a nuclear power plant that is strictly specified according to international safety regulations.

Sorting techniques typically involve stakeholders arranging some statements according to their agreement with them. For example, you can ask stakeholders to indicate which of the following two statements they most agree with: *the project deliverables must be delivered on time*, or *the specifications for the deliverables cannot be changed*. For *complex comparisons*, you can create a range of cards with two statements, and for each card let the stakeholder choose the one with which the stakeholder agrees the most. How the stakeholders prioritize the various options can then be derived from the stakeholders' choices. If there are *many alternatives* to evaluate, you can simplify the task by first asking the stakeholder to sort cards with statements into three or five groups, e.g. from *strongly agree* to *strongly disagree* or from *very important* to *not at all important*.

Sorting requires relatively few resources from stakeholders to uncover their preferences and – perhaps more interestingly – it provides an opportunity to talk about the prioritization that stakeholders make while sorting takes place. Therefore, sorting techniques work best if the activity involves several stakeholders at the same time.

## Take care of your data

Primary data is tailored to your need for information, and there may be positive side effects from the interaction you have with stakeholders when collecting data using interactive methods. Collecting primary data can be very resource-intensive and requires knowledge of research methods, e.g. how to conduct a personal or focus group interview, facilitate a workshop, conduct a questionnaire survey or conduct a structured observation. Therefore, consider if you can find some of the data that you need in the project documents and other existing data sources. It is important to consider this before you start collecting primary data. However, not all data can be found in documents, especially information about what is on the stakeholders' minds. For that, the advantages of primary data, especially collected in interaction with the stakeholders, are such that we recommend that you allocate resources to collecting such data. If you lack the competence to do this yourself, you can use a trained and well-prepared interviewer or workshop facilitator.

It is a challenge that some of the information that the project obtains in the stakeholder analysis may be personal and perhaps even sensitive and therefore not suitable for being written in documents that are distributed to a wider audience. You must therefore decide what information you write down and the level of detail that is necessary. When collecting data about stakeholders in Europe, you must always remember the General Data Protection Regulation (GDPR) principles. The most important ones are that you may only collect the information that you need to use; that you must inform about what you will use the information for; that you only use the information for what you have informed about; and that you store the information properly and not longer than you have informed about.

**Mini-case 7 Meeting the daunting stakeholders**

A project manager at a public health institution carried out an internal change project. She was inexperienced in project management and therefore insecure in that role. It aggravated the situation that some of the stakeholders were at a high managerial level in the organization and had high-ranking jobs. The project manager believed that these stakeholders would be against the project. She was afraid that in a dialogue with them, she would fall completely short and that they would become even more negative about the project. and would think that she wasted their time. She therefore avoided having contact with them. However, she reluctantly agreed to interview the frightening and negative stakeholders when she participated in a research project on project managers' stakeholder management. To her great surprise, the "scary" stakeholders were very happy to talk about the project, and they gave very positive feedback on being heard and listened to. This had a positive impact on the project and helped its survival and progress.

Source: Interviews and workshops conducted by the authors. The case is anonymized

*It is tempting to keep your distance from stakeholders who frighten you, especially if you are in general very busy with other stakeholders and urgent tasks.*

*The case illustrates that it can be beneficial for a project manager to overcome this barrier and collect primary data through interaction with the stakeholders, even if the project manager is not trained to do so.*

*The case also illustrates that a dialogue with stakeholders with a negative attitude can have a positive impact. It is the project manager's job to think about engagement of all identified stakeholders, including the frightening ones. It is important that it is a conscious and – for the project – strategic choice if the project manager chooses not to contact some of the stakeholders.*

## References

Chung, K. S. K., Eskerod, P., Jepsen, A. L., & Zhang, J. (2023). Response strategies for community stakeholder engagement on social media: A case study of a large infrastructure project. *International Journal of Project Management*, 41 (5), 102495.

Clegg, D., & Barker, R. (1994). *Case method fast-track: A RAD approach.* Addison-Wesley.

Huemann, M., Eskerod, P., & Ringhofer, C. (2016). *Rethink project stakeholder management.* Project Management Institute.

Jepsen, A. L., & Eskerod, P. (2009). Stakeholder analysis in projects: Challenges in using current guidelines in the real world. *International Journal of Project Management*, 27 (4), 335–343.

Mariani, C., Navrotska, Y., & Mancini, M. (2023). Unsupervised machine learning for project stakeholder classification: Benefits and limitations. *Project Leadership and Society*, 4, 100093.

Wack, P. (1985). Scenarios: Uncharted waters ahead. *Harvard Business Review*, 63 (5), 73–89.

# 8 Stakeholder engagement

Once you have determined which stakeholders you need to engage and the potential challenges involved, you are ready to plan your stakeholder engagement. The need for engagement differs across stakeholders. It also varies for the same stakeholder depending on the issue and the project phase. Some stakeholders need a close dialogue and frequent interactions to ensure their contributions or to take their interests into account. Others may simply need to follow the progress of the project.

You should choose an overall approach for engaging the project stakeholders, so that there is a common thread in your actions. You also need to decide your approach to planning your engagement efforts: will you spend resources on engaging stakeholders proactively to avoid conflicts and other challenges, or do you prefer to react to problems, should they arise? When you plan your efforts to avoid problems, you need to decide which strategy you will use towards each stakeholder, and how you will put the strategy into play, as well as the specific actions that you want to set in motion. Finally, you need to think about possible reactions to problems that materialize despite your efforts to avoid them. How to go about these things is the subject of this chapter.

## Approaches to engagement and planning

You can conduct stakeholder engagement with a *collaborative* or a *power-oriented* approach. Project managers with a collaborative approach try to get the project going through dialogue. They try to meet the stakeholder's requirements or find solutions that benefit

DOI: 10.4324/9781003712695-8

both parties. If this is not possible, they try to find a solution where the stakeholders experience the fewest possible disadvantages overall. A project manager with a power-oriented approach will use pressure to persuade the stakeholders to contribute. Your approach will often contain elements of both collaboration and use of power, as it is generally advantageous to combine the two approaches. For example, you can invite your stakeholders to contribute while at the same time pressuring them to do so, e.g. by pointing out the negative financial influence if the project fails to progress as planned.

We recommend *collaboration as far as possible* for several reasons. First, a one-sided power-oriented approach fails to agree with modern principles of management. It is contrary to social responsibility and sustainability. Second, a power-oriented approach assumes that you have power over the stakeholder, e.g. through formal management authority or the ability to reward and sanction the stakeholder. A project manager rarely has this option. Third, a power-oriented approach is ineffective because the compliance, which you achieve by using power, only lasts when the stakeholders believe that you will notice if they fail to comply. Therefore, with a power-oriented approach, resources must be spent on demonstrating that you have power and on monitoring whether the stakeholders contribute as needed.

Collaboration with the stakeholder with the aim to find the best possible solution for all is therefore a better way. This is in line with the *managing for stakeholders approach* presented in Chapter 2. However, finding good solutions for all through collaboration is not always straightforward. Each stakeholder has requirements and wishes, and these may not coincide with, or they may even conflict with, the requirements and wishes of other stakeholders. Therefore, you will probably not be able to meet all requirements and wishes. At some point, meeting one stakeholder's requirements or wishes comes at the expense of another stakeholder's requirements and wishes. You must then make trade-offs and decide to what extent the individual stakeholder's requirements and wishes can be met. You must also try to influence the stakeholders to accept your solution, and if this is not possible, perhaps force them to accept it.

It is important that you make the trade-offs so that the project's progress and thus the value for the base organization are supported as far as possible while destroying as little value as possible for the stakeholders. For example, a construction project may require work outside normal working hours to be completed on time. Unfortunately, working late in the evening and at night can disrupt the neighbours' sleep. To minimize this problem, the project can agree on a delay with the customer to limit the work to 6am–10pm rather than 24 hours a day. The project here makes a trade-off between how quickly the customer can get their delivery and thus the time that the project can finish, and the neighbours' sleep.

Along with deciding on the balance between a collaborative or a power-oriented approach, you need to decide whether your engagement of each stakeholder will be primarily *proactive* or *reactive*. *Proactive* stakeholder engagement involves trying to predict to what extent a given stakeholder will contribute to the project, and, based on this, plan and act to ensure their necessary contributions, e.g. by keeping a positive stakeholder informed about progress through a newsletter. By doing so, you invest in avoiding negative consequences for the project from stakeholders not contributing as needed. *Reactive* stakeholder engagement means that you act in response to the actions and requirements of stakeholders, e.g. by communicating with a stakeholder who has expressed negative views about the project or who has requests for changes to the project.

Note that *doing nothing*, i.e. waiting to actively engage a given stakeholder or just *monitoring* (following a stakeholder), is not necessarily the same as being reactive. It may be the result of a well-considered decision not to act at present, e.g. because you consider it unnecessary, or because you believe that action is futile. Maybe you have established that a stakeholder is strongly against your project, and perhaps with good reason. In that case, it may make no sense to spend a lot of resources trying to change this stakeholder's lack of intention to contribute. Your resources are probably better spent monitoring whether the stakeholder will act on the negative opinion and only do something if negative actions materialize. A further example of a stakeholder that it is sufficient to monitor is a stakeholder who is currently positive towards the project and therefore in no need for attention.

To ensure the best possible value creation from the project, we recommend that you are generally proactive in your stakeholder engagement. It is important to understand that being proactive is a way of thinking – a mindset. It is not about conducting predefined actions. The mindset involves constantly thinking about how to best interact with your stakeholders in relation to the next actions that will take place in the project. However, be aware that you often must plan reactive actions as a supplement to the proactive actions, because they can rarely eliminate a risk.

Figure 8.1 provides an overview of the two approaches (collaborative and power-oriented) combined with the two planning mindsets (proactive and reactive). We first review proactive stakeholder engagement. After this, we turn to options for reacting if there are challenges in your stakeholder engagement.

## Proactive engagement

With proactive stakeholder engagement, you consider ahead of a situation which – if any – action is needed to ensure that each stakeholder contributes as needed. The result of the stakeholder analysis, and thus the stakeholder category that the stakeholder belongs to in relation to the expected intention to contribute to the project, provides a basis for this consideration (see Table 6.1 or the stakeholder register in Table 6.2). If a stakeholder is marked with dark or light grey because the stakeholder has a negative perception of the project or of contributing to the project, you need to work with the stakeholder – we label this that *the stakeholder needs attention.*

To plan how to give this attention and engage the stakeholders in a positive way, you need to choose an *engagement strategy* for each stakeholder, i.e. *what* challenge it is that you want to work with. To realize the strategy, you need to determine one or more *tactics* for the engagement, i.e. *how* you can engage the stakeholder via involvement in the project or via communication. Finally, you must plan the *specific*

| | Collaborative approach | Power-oriented approach |
|---|---|---|
| Proactive mindset | Prevent problems by thinking ahead with a focus on avoiding them through collaboration | Prevent problems by thinking ahead with a focus on how to pressure stakeholders to contribute |
| Reactive mindset | Solve problems as they arise in collaboration with relevant stakeholders | Solve problems as they arise by pushing stakeholders to contribute |

*Figure 8.1* Engagement approaches and planning mindsets

*actions* that are to take place, e.g. information meetings, information flyers, etc. As a part of this, you need to design your *communication efforts*, which we elaborate on in Chapter 9. We recommend that you document your decisions in an *engagement plan*, which we will explain in Chapter 10.

When engaging project stakeholders, there are basically *four situations, each with a different challenge* that you can work with. For each challenge, a different *engagement strategy* is relevant. The *first situation* is that the stakeholder is reluctant to contribute because of a negative attitude towards contributing in general or towards the act needed for a specific contribution. In this case, a relevant engagement strategy is to influence the attitude in a positive direction or to induce the stakeholder to contribute despite the negative attitude. The *second situation* is that the stakeholder is reluctant to contribute as necessary without being against the project or against doing the act needed for a specific contribution, e.g. providing resources. In this situation, a relevant strategy is to activate the potential to influence the project positively. The *third situation* is that the stakeholder contemplates to influence the project in a negative way, e.g. by withholding resources. In this situation, a relevant strategy is to reduce the stakeholder's potential to influence negatively. Finally, in the *fourth situation*, there is no challenge. In this situation, the stakeholder can be expected to contribute to the project as needed, and therefore there is no need to plan actions towards the stakeholder. The strategy is thus to maintain the current state.

Table 8.1 shows the four engagement strategies and the stakeholder categories that they are relevant for. Note that *multiple strategies may be relevant* towards the same stakeholder. We recommend that you choose the strategy that addresses the situation that poses the greatest challenge and pursue it first.

The strategy is a general approach for what it is that you will work on in relation to each stakeholder. To plan your stakeholder engagement, you need to decide on the ways you will work to realize the strategy and the specific actions that you want to set in motion. Table 8.2 provides suggestions for engagement tactics with possible actions for each strategy. We now expand on the four strategies with relevant engagement tactics and possible actions.

We start with the first strategy, which is to *influence the stakeholder's attitude in a positive direction or apply pressure to set the negative*

*Table 8.1* Situations, stakeholder categories, and engagement strategies

| *No.* | *Situation* | *Stakeholder category* | *Engagement strategy* |
|---|---|---|---|
| 1 | The stakeholder has a negative attitude towards contributing to the project in general or towards doing the act needed for a specific contribution | Negative key player<br>Negative resourceful<br>Negative showstopper<br>Negative marginal | *Influence* the stakeholder's attitude in a positive direction or apply pressure to set the negative attitude aside |
| 2 | The stakeholder is reluctant to contribute as needed but does not have a negative attitude towards contributing | Neutral or positive key player<br>Neutral or positive resourceful | *Activate* the stakeholder's potential to influence positively |
| 3 | The stakeholder can be expected to influence the project negatively | Negative key player<br>Negative showstopper | *Reduce* the stakeholder's potential to influence negatively |
| 4 | No challenge – the stakeholder is positive and can be expected to contribute as needed | Positive key player<br>Positive resourceful<br>Positive showstopper<br>Positive marginal | *Maintain* the stakeholder in the current state |

*Table 8.2* Engagement strategies with examples of tactics and actions

| *Strategy* | *Tactics* | *Actions* |
|---|---|---|
| *Influence* the stakeholder's attitude in a positive direction or apply pressure to set the negative attitude aside | Change the actual consequences of contributing (benefits and costs, personal relevance)<br>Change expectations<br>Improve the perception of fairness<br>Put pressure on the stakeholder to act despite expected negative consequences | Inform about consequences<br>Include stakeholder proposals in planning<br>Put pressure on the stakeholder<br>Highlight possible negative consequences of not contributing<br>Draw attention to expectations of the role or to others' (positive) attitude to the stakeholder's participation<br>Assign formal project role |

| *Strategy* | *Tactics* | *Actions* |
|---|---|---|
| *Activate* the stakeholder's potential to influence positively | Improve the ability to act<br>In case of low control over the decision to participate, obtain support for participation<br>Appeal to pressure from social norms to overcome insecurity<br>Push to activate action | Give instruction<br>Use role models<br>Draw attention to expectations of the role or to others' (positive) attitude to the stakeholder's participation<br>Talk to the stakeholder's manager<br>Give order to action<br>Assign formal project role |
| *Reduce* the stakeholder's potential to influence negatively | Reduce the power base<br>Expand your own power base | Network<br>Identify substitutes<br>Make sure that there are alternative participants or suppliers |
| *Maintain* the stakeholder in the current state | Keep informed<br>Await developments<br>Support the positive perception of contributing<br>Support the perception of fairness | Communicate progress and results<br>Assign formal project role, e.g. in reference group<br>Include stakeholder proposals in planning<br>Acknowledge support and influence |

*attitude aside.* This is relevant if the stakeholder's attitude towards the project or towards doing the act needed to contribute is negative. Returning to Table 5.1, we see that a possible tactic to change this could be to *change the actual consequences of contributing*, i.e. what the stakeholder gets out of contributing in relation to what the stakeholder must invest in contributing. This can be done by addressing the stakeholder's concerns and reducing any negative side effects by adapting the project. You can also increase the benefits from contributing, e.g. by giving the stakeholder a reward for contributing, such as influence or financial compensation. Or you can lower the costs by making it easier for the stakeholder to contribute, through good guidance or clear descriptions of what you need from the stakeholder.

Another possible tactic to influence the stakeholder's attitude in a positive direction is to *change expectations.* This is relevant if the stakeholder's expectations deviate from what is really needed. You can change expectations through information about the project. If the stakeholder is important, you may want to ensure that the stakeholder is always informed by giving the stakeholder a formal project role. A formal project role will also support the perception of fairness because the stakeholder's contribution is formally recognized. If you decide to work with the stakeholder's expectations, remember that it is dangerous to create expectations that do not hold up. This will spill over into the next project. In other words, you must be very careful not to create unrealistic expectations about the benefits or costs of contributing.

You can also influence the stakeholder to *set the negative attitude aside* by *applying pressure to set the negative attitude aside*, i.e. pointing out if an action is expected from the role of the stakeholder in the project. For example, a project owner who is negative towards bringing up an issue at a higher level in the organization can be pressured to do so with reference to the duties of a project owner. Another type of pressure is to introduce or augment the costs of a lack of contributing, e.g. by telling the stakeholder that the benefits will be reduced, or the costs will be increased if the agreed contribution is not delivered as planned. If a supplier fails to deliver on time and to the agreed quality, they may not get paid – or may be asked to pay the extra transportation costs if a delivery is split into two instead of one. It can sometimes be an advantage if such consequences are explicit, agreed, and documented in the contract between the stakeholder and the project at the beginning of the project. Other types of pressure are vague and indirect. They can consist of telling stories that illustrate to the stakeholder that their behaviour is considered unacceptable, or that the stakeholder's benefits will be reduced, either in the specific project or in potential future projects in the base organization, if the stakeholder fails to cooperate.

Furthermore, you can consider if the stakeholder is negative towards doing the act because of a negative *perception of fairness* in the project. For example, an employee may be against the introduction of a new machine that automates some work processes. If most colleagues think the new machine is helpful, the negative employee may choose to accept the introduction of the new machine.

The second strategy is to *activate the stakeholder's potential to influence* the project *positively*. This strategy is particularly relevant if the stakeholder is mainly hesitant to contribute due to low perceived ability to act because of a perceived lack of skills. If this is the case, a sensible tactic is to *improve the ability to act* by instructing the stakeholder how it is possible to contribute, e.g. by having a role model demonstrate how to do it, such as showing how to register for a meeting, go there, and participate. Another situation is that the stakeholder lacks support from management to contribute as needed. In this situation, you can augment the ability to act by ensuring this support.

Still another situation is that the stakeholder is positive and wants to contribute but fails to do so at the relevant time or to do the act at all. This means that *an intention does not become action*. This could be, for example, if the stakeholder is to contribute by writing and submitting a report, but there are signs that this will not happen on time. In this case, the tactic could be to *push the stakeholder* to work on the report so that it will be finished on time. It may be that a reminder that it is now is a sufficient action.

If the issue is rather insecurity than ability to act, the tactic could be *to apply pressure from social norms to overcome the insecurity* by pointing out the appropriateness of contributing. You can appeal directly or indirectly to the stakeholder – "you should do this". Remember that you can only use coercive pressure on stakeholders with little potential to negatively influence the project. Powerful stakeholders who are pressured may choose to retaliate and thus threaten the project and its ability to create the desired results.

The third strategy is to *reduce the stakeholder's potential to negatively influence the project*. This may be relevant if you are concerned that a stakeholder will use their opportunity to negatively impact the project, and you think that it is difficult to change the underlying attitude or set it aside by application of social pressure. A tactic is to *reduce the stakeholder's power base*. Sometimes you will be able to adapt the project so that the stakeholder's contribution is no longer as necessary. Other times you can find alternatives to the stakeholder, e.g. other suppliers or other employees with the same expertise. Another tactic is to reduce the relative opportunity to negatively impact the project by *strengthening your own power base*. You can do this through networking of various kinds. This can even be with persons who are in the stakeholder's network, including their superiors.

The fourth strategy is to *maintain the stakeholder in the current state*. If the stakeholder is positive, and you assume that the stakeholder will continue to be so, a relevant tactic is to *wait*, i.e. do nothing, apart from keeping an eye on the stakeholder. If you believe that the stakeholder's positive intention to contribute needs support, you can provide arguments that *justify the positive intention*. You can also *support the perception of fairness* in the way the project is managed, e.g. by regularly informing the stakeholder and verbalizing any support from the stakeholder so that they feel recognized. If the stakeholder is a key player, it may be relevant to assign them a formal project role, e.g. in a steering committee or a reference group. Note that maintaining the current state requires some effort, at least to keep an eye on whether the stakeholder feels disadvantaged compared to more challenging stakeholders. If a positive key player notices that a negative showstopper is getting extra benefits for being satisfied, the key player may feel overlooked and treated unfairly. This may cause his or her intention to contribute to change from positive to negative.

Several of the actions in Table 8.2 involve stakeholders in *dialogues and negotiations* about matters such as the project's purpose, deliverables, and scope. Sharing professional knowledge, relevant experiences, and preferences among and with the stakeholders is an important way to increase the overall understanding of the entire project and its conditions. Knowledge sharing can also help align expectations, especially in the project initiation and planning phases. In this context, it is important to mention that there can be *too much stakeholder engagement*. Dialogues and negotiations take time, not only for you but also for the stakeholders and can lead to lengthy discussions. This can cause delays, increase complexity, or create expectations that you cannot meet. This can happen, for example, if you conduct workshops to collect suggestions for solutions in a change project where you can only use a few of the suggestions. Then some of the workshop participants may be disappointed because they expected that their suggestions would make a difference in the project. In addition, involvement can be tiring for all parties.

On the other hand, *too little stakeholder engagement* can lead to misunderstandings and dissatisfied stakeholders – and ultimately to the project not generating the greatest possible value for all. If you save yourself the hassle of involving and negotiating with stakeholders at the beginning of the project, you may run into problems later. Time spent getting off to a good start in relations with stakeholders can pave the way for the project. This is because stakeholders, through involvement, get a realistic picture of each other and align expectations – unless, of course, the negotiations reveal such major discrepancies that the project cannot move forward.

Table 8.3 continues the example from Table 6.2. As an example, we take a closer look at the union representative. It is enough that the union representative, who is a key player, is neither positive nor negative. Therefore, the project manager chooses the strategy to maintain the stakeholder in the current state. The project manager chooses to apply the tactics to support the positive perception of contributing and a positive perception of fairness. The project manager chooses to support the positive perception of contributing through information on an ongoing basis. The project manager can do this, because she can point to a wide range of positive consequences of the action, e.g. that challenges among employees will be taken care of through training. The project manager supports the perception of fairness through recognition of the essential role of the union representative by giving him a formal role in a reference group that will follow the project, and which therefore meets at the project's important milestones.

## Reactive engagement

Although you should be proactive in your stakeholder engagement, it is necessary to know some reactive tactics because sometimes it may be necessary to react in response to, for example, unforeseen requirements from stakeholders, in connection with a conflict, or in a crisis. Or you may have seen a stakeholder as so unpredictable that you have chosen not to plan proactive actions and hope that the stakeholder refrains from harming the project, and now the stakeholder acts in a way that requires your reaction.

Table 8.4 shows, based on Aaltonen and Sivonen (2009), five different reactive tactics along with possible actions. The first tactic is to *adapt* the project to stakeholder requirements. This could be, for example, delivering faster than planned if a customer suddenly needs the deliverable. Complying with the stakeholder's requirements may be the best solution if a stakeholder has a high potential to negatively influence the project – key players and showstoppers.

If you cannot meet the stakeholder's requirements, or it is very costly to do so, it may be better to opt for a *compromise*, e.g. refraining from doing construction work later than a certain time of the day

*Table 8.3* Example of engagement strategy, tactics, and actions

| *Stakeholder with category* | *Challenges and opportunities* | *Strategy* | *Engagement tactics* | *Planned actions* |
|---|---|---|---|---|
| Project owner – positive key player | May lose interest as the project progresses | Maintain the stakeholder in the current state | Support the perception of fairness | Communicate progress and results at project status meetings |
| Union representative – key player (neither positive nor negative) | Can be challenged by negative employees | Maintain the stakeholder in the current state | Support the positive perception of contributing<br>Support the perception of fairness | Inform on an ongoing basis<br>Formal role in the project: member of reference group |
| Negative employees – marginals, but as group key player | May be worried if their skills suffice with the new work tasks<br>Can team up with other negative members | Influence attitude in a positive direction | Change the expectation of how the new action influences the work processes | Inform about consequences<br>Include stakeholder proposals in planning |

*Table 8.4* Reactive tactics

| *Tactic* | *Examples of actions* |
|---|---|
| Adapt | Adapt to the requirements and wishes of the stakeholder |
| Compromise | Negotiate with the stakeholder<br>Clarify and communicate what it takes to meet the requirements and wishes, as well as the consequences of doing so, e.g. increased costs for the stakeholder or delays<br>Lobby to change or perhaps completely avoid the stakeholder's requirements and wishes<br>Listen to the stakeholder's requirements, wishes, and, not least, concerns<br>Offer more planned benefits<br>Reduce stakeholder costs<br>Offer influence |
| Ignore | Defer reaction (indefinitely)<br>Don't react on a request |
| Reject | Say no to the stakeholder's requirements and wishes<br>Refer to previous agreements and the project plan<br>Refer to others who can solve the problem<br>Provide detailed reasons for the rejection |
| Conflict resolution | Conduct a resolution dialogue<br>Conduct a third-party dialogue<br>Escalate issue<br>Conduct a termination dialogue |

Source: Inspired by Aaltonen and Sivonen (2009)

if it turns out that it influences the neighbours more than anticipated in the planning phase.

If a stakeholder can be classified as marginal or resourceful because they are unable to negatively influence the project, it may be an option to *ignore* a possible request or to postpone an answer – perhaps indefinitely. Another option is to *reject* the stakeholder's requirements. If you choose to use one of these two tactics, remember that it can negatively influence the project if you treat stakeholders in a way that is perceived by others as unfair, as we discussed in Chapter 5. You should therefore consider the urgency and the legitimacy of the stakeholder's request.

The fifth reactive tactic, *conflict resolution* (Zartman, 2007), is relevant if the challenges with a stakeholder have not been resolved through one of the other four tactics. You need a conflict resolution if something has happened that could seriously hinder the progress of the project, and communication with the stakeholders has broken down so that negotiation towards a compromise is no longer possible. Conflict resolution can then take place through a *resolution dialogue* where you collaborate and focus on the future tasks in the project. In the resolution dialogue, it is important that you respect the stakeholder's own problem-solving abilities and resources. This means that you must listen to the stakeholder's proposed solutions. It is also important to avoid getting too involved in the past and the circumstances, e.g. differences in personality types or communication styles that may be the cause of the problems in the collaborative relationship. A *third-party dialogue*, i.e. using a mediator, is another option. Here you ask a neutral person outside the project to facilitate the dialogue and act as a mediator.

*Issue escalation* to a higher level in the organization is a third option that is relevant if you need support from the base organization or the stakeholder's organization. It is useful to consider early in the project who should be involved if a crisis occurs and incorporate this into an issue escalation plan. This can save time in a critical situation. It may also be wise to ask some of the stakeholders, e.g. important customers, to prepare an issue escalation plan with specified decision-making processes and communication channels in their organization, so that communication can take place as quickly as possible, and with the right people, in the event of a crisis in the project. Issues are escalated because a decision-maker at a higher level has more decision-making competence and perhaps also more knowledge about the strategic opportunities in the organization, which he or she can contribute to the decision-making process. In addition, escalation can give a positive signal: "We really take this issue seriously, and therefore we are willing to involve persons at a higher organizational level to find a solution".

Sometimes the conflict is so serious that the relationship with the stakeholder cannot survive. In this case, you may need to invite the stakeholder to a *termination dialogue*, which involves explaining to the stakeholder, face to face, why the collaboration must end. Termination dialogues are not possible with all stakeholders. They are most relevant when there is a contractual obligation, such as with a customer or a supplier. A lawsuit is of course also an option in that situation.

## Get ahead of the curve with proactive engagement

It can be tempting to resort to quick fixes and pressure stakeholders to contribute or, at the other extreme, do nothing and hope for the best. Small challenges with stakeholders can, however, turn into big challenges. Therefore, it is a good investment to spend resources on a collaborative approach with proactive tactics and suitable actions adapted to the challenges of the individual stakeholder or group of stakeholders.

**Mini-case 8 Leave it to the consultant versus hand in hand**

A municipality established a project to develop a new branding concept for the municipality. It outsourced all project management and stakeholder engagement to an experienced consultancy firm. The consultancy firm used many resources on workshops with various stakeholders, including members of the city council, business owners, and associations. However, not all invited attended the workshops, e.g. an influential member of the city council.

The consultancy firm used the knowledge that they gained from the workshops uncritically in the development of the new branding concept. When doing so, they failed to notice that the influential city councillor, who stayed away from their workshops, was against the developed branding concept. And they were unaware that the councillor discussed his opposition with other members of the city council and managed to turn several councillors against their branding concept.

When the project presented the new branding concept to the city council before moving on to the next step, the city council denied continuation of the project in its present form, which surprised the consultancy company immensely.

The result was that the consultancy company completely lost its legitimacy and could not complete the project. After some discussion, the city council decided that the municipality should appoint an internal project manager for the project, while the consulting company agreed to replace their consultant.

The new consultant and the internal project manager then conducted a joint round of visits to the key stakeholders. After these efforts, the project was finally back on track.

Source: Interviews, observations, and workshops conducted by one of the authors. The case is anonymized

*The case illustrates that a project may need reactive engagement methods even though the project manager has proactively planned stakeholder engagement. Even experienced, external project managers can overlook important stakeholders and forget to keep track of how the stakeholders see and act in relation to the project.*

*The case also illustrates that it can help an external project manager to get support from an internal resourceful stakeholder who has a network and knowledge of the stakeholders, and who can follow the situation through his or her daily work in the organization.*

## References

Aaltonen, K., & Sivonen, R. (2009). Response strategies to stakeholder pressures in global projects. *International Journal of Project Management*, 27 (2), 131–141.

Zartman, I. W. (2007). *Negotiation and conflict management: Essays on theory and practice*. Routledge.

# 9 Communication efforts

Stakeholder engagement will always involve communication to and with the stakeholders. It is important that this is planned well, because a poorly planned communication effort can limit knowledge sharing between the stakeholders and the project. Badly distributed information can lead to stakeholders lacking relevant information when they need it, or that sensitive information is revealed to the wrong people. Communication that is formulated in a way so that stakeholders find it relevant and can understand it can prevent misunderstandings and disappointments as well as wrong perceptions of the project and the needed contributions. The project and the project stakeholders thus need well-planned communication, and therefore you, together with your project owner, must answer the following questions (Eskerod & Jepsen, 2016):

- What is your communication need, and what are the limitations?
- How do you want to present your message – what should your means be?
- Who will communicate the message?
- Where will the communication take place – what media will you use to get in touch with stakeholders?
- When and how often will the communication take place?

The considerations associated with each question are the subjects of this chapter.

DOI: 10.4324/9781003712695-9

## What is your communication need and what are the limitations?

It is important to identify your need for communication with the stakeholders across the project course. You also need to consider the limitations within which you must plan your communication, such as budget, legislation, and organizational constraints.

The stakeholder register provides the foundation for deciding your communication efforts in relation to each stakeholder, as it has information on the stakeholder's need for attention as well as the foundation for this need. In addition, the engagement strategy and tactics should guide the communication activities that you set in motion. Notice that some communication is needed by only a single or a few stakeholders, e.g. when a specific contribution is needed, while some communication is relevant for many stakeholders about, for example, the project's purpose, scope, budget, and progress.

Most importantly, you need to make sure that all stakeholders have a shared understanding of the project and its purpose. To this end, you should facilitate a decision of an *overall message* that covers the purpose of the project. This message must be relevant for all stakeholders. It is important that the message is clear and simple, and that the wording is easy to understand – like a slogan. It is a good idea to create a project title that contains the message or a very short version of the message. This can be in the form of an acronym, which is a word formed from the initial letters, e.g. CHOICES (which is an acronym for Childhood Obesity Intervention Cost-Effectiveness Study).

It is often relevant to supplement the overall message with one or more sub-messages clarifying various sub-purposes of the project that are relevant for different stakeholders. In connection with CHOICES, you can, for example, focus more on how to buy healthy food with a low income in the communication targeted at parents, and on enjoying healthy meals in the communication targeted at children.

When communicating different messages to different stakeholders, and possibly the same message in different ways to different stakeholders, you need to make sure not to contradict yourself. Contradictory messages can easily undermine your credibility. An example is a health promotion project in a company, where the aim is to reduce the costs of sick leave. In such a project, it can be tempting to use different messages to different stakeholders in the organization. It can be tempting to emphasize the cost reduction to top management, an improved well-being to employees, and a strengthened image to the HR department. It is problematic to use such diverging messages because employees and the HR department can easily uncover the real purpose of the project.

Box 9.1 offers a summary of what to communicate.

**Box 9.1 What to communicate**

- Define your need for communication with each stakeholder
- Create a general message and possibly sub-messages that briefly summarize the project's purpose and sub-purposes
- Make sure that sub-messages are congruent
- Maybe create an acronym for the project

It is one thing to know what and how much you want to communicate. It is another to know what is possible within the *contractual agreements* and the *financial constraints* that have been set in the project mandate. You need to consider these when planning your communication efforts. However, bear in mind that you may be able to renegotiate the budget later, when you can be precise on the resources that you need to execute a good communication plan.

*Legislation* may also set constraints, e.g. by requiring certain forms of communication, such as consultations with stakeholders. In addition, the base organization may have a *communication policy* that restricts what you are allowed to do. It may prohibit emailing a broad group of stakeholders or require that mass communication shows certain types of variation in the use of role models or in images, e.g. in relation to age, gender, and ethnicity.

## How will you communicate?

Once you have determined your need for communication, you must decide how you will communicate to get your message through to your stakeholders in a convincing way. You can use verbal forms such as text or speech to convey information or narratives, or non-verbal forms such as images, possibly with symbolic content. You can decide to present only the positive sides of the project, or you can present pros and cons, including negative side effects. You need to find out what works best for each issue and for stakeholders with different characteristics.

Reading information in text form requires more involvement of the recipient than feeling an emotion when looking at an image. The *Elaboration Likelihood Model* (ELM) (Petty et al., 1983) states that you need to consider this when planning your communication with recipients with different levels of involvement. ELM states that individuals who are *involved* – or *committed*, using the McElroy and Mills (2003) framework – are willing to use more cognitive capacity to learn about the issue. Stakeholders with a strongly negative or positive commitment towards the project or towards making the necessary contributions are involved. They are interested in the issue and want to spend time gaining knowledge about it. Stakeholders with a neutral commitment are uninvolved – they don't care. Therefore, they don't feel a need for information about the consequences of the project or the potential consequences of contributing. This means that they are also unwilling to devote resources to receiving and processing information about the project or contribution – from their perspective, they don't get anything out of it.

Because the uninvolved stakeholders lack willingness to spend resources on receiving and understanding communication, you need to use what Petty et al. (1983) label the *peripheral route to persuasion*, where persuasion can be equated with *influence*. Via the peripheral route, influence occurs through learning a simple association between something (e.g. the project) and inducing a nice feeling (e.g. happy employees) by *repeatedly* connecting the two. This type of learning is referred to as *classical conditioning* (Pavlov, 1927), which often uses *non-verbal communication* (Petty et al., 1983) to present the repeated message. For example, to repeatedly display a message about the purpose of the project together with a thumbs up or a positive slogan such as "New roads around the hospital – a benefit for you". The thumbs up and the slogan signals something positive. A recipient – a stakeholder – who sees the combination many times learns a positive association between the project and the positive signals.

You can combine classical conditioning with *operant conditioning* (Skinner, 1938), which also only requires few resources to process. Operant conditioning creates and supports a positive association with an action by *rewarding* the action. It can also support a negative association with not contributing by *sanctioning* a lack of contribution, e.g. by stating the missing contribution in shared meeting minutes or a project status report. You can reward a stakeholder for contributing by, for example, thanking them for their contribution. You can also reward indirectly by having role models talk about having received something positive (a reward) from contributing to the project. For example, you can show a role model such as a typical citizen who talks about the benefits that came from participating in an information meeting about the project. Likewise, a role model can talk about a necessary piece of information that the person would have received at a meeting that the person failed to attend. Rewards can be financial or in other forms, such as a positive experience or recognition. Rewards support the stakeholder in the perception that it was a good idea to contribute. They help create a positive attitude towards contributing and can encourage the stakeholder to contribute again.

Influence via the peripheral route is particularly relevant for maintaining a positive attitude among stakeholders who are not particularly committed, such as some positive key players, resourcefuls, and showstoppers. Communication via the peripheral route can generally help to create awareness of the project or an issue and thereby activate a potential to positively influence the project among stakeholders with low commitment to enhance their motivation to invest resources in receiving and understanding communication about the project.

If a stakeholder has a strong opinion about a project or a specific issue, the stakeholder is *involved*. In this situation, it is possible to influence the stakeholder via the *direct (or central) route to influence* by application of *cognitive learning* where the stakeholder is influenced through verbal communication (e.g. dialogue or printed information) that explains the value that the project will bring or the benefits from contributing. Because the stakeholder is involved, he or she is motivated to learn something about the project. This means that you can enter a dialogue with the stakeholder about the project. In this dialogue you can discuss expected and actual benefits and costs as well as possible side effects orally or in writing. You can direct the communication towards *influencing the attitude towards doing the act (and thus contributing)* of negative stakeholders. You can also *maintain the attitude of positive stakeholders* through information on the positive value from the project or benefits from contributing. This is relevant if the positive attitude is under attack from negative stakeholders. Table 9.1 summarizes when it is advantageous to use the direct or the peripheral route to influence, and how the choice of route influences how you should present your message.

In the section above, we have primarily given examples of information that displays the positive side of the project and contributing. Such communication works best for maintaining a *positive attitude.* If your stakeholder has a *negative attitude*, you need communication that *addresses both possible negative and positive consequences* to influence the attitude in a positive direction (Eisend, 2007). Communication aimed at addressing a stakeholder's *negative attitude* should *acknowledge the stakeholder's concerns while pointing out the expected positive effects of the project* or *explain why the concerns are unnecessary* if they are rooted in false expectations or assumptions.

If a stakeholder has a negative attitude due to concerns about disadvantages and costs, you need to address and acknowledge this in your communication with the stakeholder. The same applies if a stakeholder is concerned that others, e.g. colleagues, are against the stakeholder's contribution to the project. In other words, you need to remove the

*Table 9.1* Direct and peripheral route to influence

| | *Route to influence* | *Learning model* | *Presenting the message* |
|---|---|---|---|
| The stakeholder is not involved in (committed to) the project | Peripheral | Classical conditioning | Repeat a simple message with a positive content |
| | | Operant conditioning | Show how desired behaviour will be rewarded or lack of desired behaviour sanctioned |
| The stakeholder is involved in (committed to) the project and interested in getting information | Direct | Cognitive | Explain verbally the advantages (and disadvantages) of the project |

Sources: Based on Pavlov (1927), Petty et al. (1983), and Skinner (1938)

background for the negative attitude before, or at the same time as, you build a positive attitude based on the benefits of the project. For example, a union representative may be negative about a change project because the union representative believes that management has bad intentions with the project. In this situation, it may be difficult to obtain collaboration from the union representative to find good solutions that will be accepted by the employees. Therefore, the project manager needs to start out by working towards a common understanding with the union representative about the intention of the change project, e.g. by informing about how the project has incorporated support for employees who are influenced by the changes in a negative way. After that, the union representative may be willing to help the project without further encouragement.

Related to this topic is whether you are communicating with a stakeholder who is knowledgeable about the issue at hand or with a stakeholder who is uninformed. Figure 9.1 shows a categorization by attitude and knowledge. Each stakeholder can be placed in one of four categories: *positive well-informed*, *negative well-informed*, *positive uninformed*, and *negative uninformed*.

A stakeholder who is a *negative uninformed* should be treated differently than a negative stakeholder who has detailed knowledge about the project and therefore is a *negative well-informed*. The latter may be a grassroots organization that is strongly opposed to the project. Providing more information probably won't help. But you may

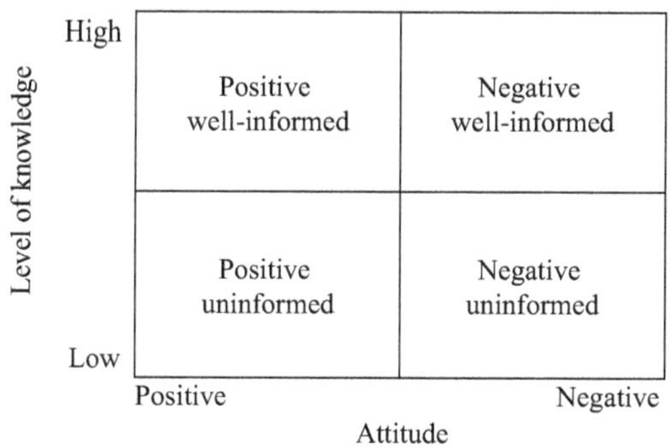


*Figure 9.1* Attitude-knowledge matrix
Source: Based on Eskerod and Jepsen (2016)

be able to influence a neighbour to a construction site in a positive direction through information on project plans, if the neighbour is protesting about the noise from the construction based on a belief that the project will take much longer than planned. Information about the project's schedule may remove some of the stakeholder's insecurity and thereby make the stakeholder less negative. Information may even prevent dissatisfied neighbours from gathering in a joint protest about the noise.

We have up to now described how you must address the communication need with each stakeholder. However, it will be too resource-demanding to create tailored communication to all stakeholders about all issues. Therefore, it can be an advantage to group your stakeholders into *segments*, understood as stakeholders who have the same need for communication, and to target your communication at these segments instead of individual stakeholders. Communication can also address several segments at a time, e.g. *stakeholders with different levels of involvement* by joint use of the *central and the peripheral routes to persuasion.* Consider a poster with images and a slogan together with text giving further explanation and information or directing the reader to more information. The *uninvolved* stakeholder is exposed to the images and slogan, which require few resources to receive. At the same time, *involved* stakeholders can find more information by reading the text or even seeking out the announced additional information.

## Who should communicate?

You need to make sure that your communication comes from someone who has the ability to influence the stakeholder. You therefore need to determine *who* will best convey the decided communication. Often, you, as the project manager, are not the best choice to do this. In the following section we look at why, and who would then be a good choice.

Who can influence others? Research (e.g. Ohanian, 1990) shows that a person has a greater chance of influencing another person if he or she: (1) is *similar* to the recipient of the communication, e.g. in age or role in the project; (2) has a *relevant connection* to the issue, i.e. has experienced it, has a role in relation to the issue, or an interest in it; (3) is *credible*; and (4) is *attractive.* Credibility requires that the recipient believes that the communicator has expertise and is honest and objective. Expertise can be based on knowledge or experience. Attractiveness should be understood very broadly in this context. An attractive person is someone the recipient would like to resemble or be on good terms with. This could be a person with authority, such as the CEO, or someone who the recipient looks up to because this person is further on the career path. It could also be a good colleague whom the recipient respects. Table 9.2 summarizes the characteristics of influential persons.

Why are you not always the best at communicating messages about the project as a project manager? The reason is that a project manager only possesses some of the characteristics that are needed to influence the stakeholders. The project manager has a relevant connection to the project and expertise on it. Therefore, the project manager meets requirement (2) and one element needed for credibility (3), i.e. has expertise. On the other hand, the project manager has a personal interest in promoting the project. Therefore, at least some stakeholders will believe that the project manager is not completely objective. This means that the project manager fails to meet the honesty and objectivity requirements to be regarded as credible (3). The stakeholders therefore may not fully trust a project manager, even if they generally perceive the project manager as an honest person.

*Table 9.2* Characteristics of influential persons

| *Type* | *Influence based on* | *Characterized by* |
|---|---|---|
| 1 | Similarity/identification with the communication recipient | Same demographic characteristics<br>Same knowledge or experience base<br>Same challenges |
| 2 | A relevant connection to the issue | Has experience with the issue<br>Has a role in relation to the issue<br>Has an interest in the issue |
| 3 | Credibility | Has expertise – knows something about the subject<br>Is perceived to be honest – wanting to tell the truth<br>Is perceived to be objective – communicating based on knowledge and not own interest |
| 4 | Attractiveness | Stakeholder wants to be on good terms with ...<br>Stakeholder wants to be like ... |

A further reason why the project manager may not be the best choice to influence stakeholders is that many stakeholders may not identify with the project manager (1). An end user of the project deliverables may be very different from the project manager. Therefore, end users may be sceptical of the project manager's ability to understand their needs and desires. Finally, stakeholders may not strive for a positive relationship with the project manager (4) and therefore do not feel any reason to listen to or comply with the project manager's directives. The project manager does not have the authority to reward compliant stakeholders, such as giving a payment or the opportunity of later collaboration. This can be exacerbated by the fact that project managers are only leaders of temporary organizations and therefore may not have much influence in the base organization.

All of this means that you may benefit from asking others to help communicate about the project. These could be *project spokespersons*, *role models*, or *opinion leaders*. Spokespersons, role models, and opinion leaders have similarities, but they differ in important ways. Table 9.3 shows the three different types of communicators and the characteristics that they need to possess to have an impact on a given stakeholder.

A *spokesperson* speaks openly on behalf of the project. Examples of project spokespersons include the project owner, the project manager, or someone from the project team. These individuals have a relevant connection to the topic and credibility through project expertise, but, as mentioned above, their objectivity is compromised by their responsibility for the project. A spokesperson is therefore a good choice for sharing information that requires insight in the project, but not for convincing sceptical stakeholders about the merits of the project.

The *role model* represents the stakeholder or someone the stakeholder would like to be. The role model thus has influence through similarity to the stakeholder. It can either be because the role model resembles the stakeholder as they are now, or because the role model represents a role or type of person the stakeholder would like to be. In that case, attractiveness also plays a role. Furthermore, the stakeholder must be able to imagine how the role model's experience or way of doing something can be transferred to the stakeholder. It could, for example, be a role model for a type of citizen that the project would like to attend an information meeting about a new cycle path. In that case, the role model must resemble a typical citizen.

*Table 9.3* Spokesperson, role model, and opinion leader

| | *Characteristic* | *Similarity with the recipient* | *Relevant connection to the issue* | *Credibility through* | *Attractiveness* |
|---|---|---|---|---|---|
| Spokesperson | Speaks on behalf of the project | Not necessary | A formal relationship with the project | Expertise and insider knowledge | Position, earned respect, or the way the person expresses himself |
| Role model | Represents the recipient | Must be similar to the stakeholder now, or what the stakeholder wants to become | Experience with doing the act needed to contribute | Perceived honesty and expertise in knowing how it is for this type of person | Mirroring the stakeholder |
| Opinion leader | Shares opinions or knowledge about the project | Not necessary | Interest in and knowledge about the issue | Expertise, perceived honesty, and objectivity | That the stakeholder wants to show respect or interest |

Stakeholders with positive experiences and thus relevant connections to the topic can be used as role models for other stakeholders if they are willing to share positive experiences. This could, for example, be a citizen sharing experiences from participating in project town hall meetings and the impact that their and other citizens' feedback at the meetings has had on projects. The use of role models is particularly relevant when project stakeholders are unsure whether they can help or whether the costs associated with doing so are too high. Seeing how others have done something makes it easier for a stakeholder to imagine how to do the task. Role models are therefore particularly relevant in relation to positive key players and resourcefuls, where you would like to activate a potential to positively influence the project. They can also be relevant to communicate with negative marginals because these are often ordinary citizens or users who feel poorly represented in the project, and who may be sceptical towards spokespersons.

An *opinion leader* is motivated to express their own opinion about the project or an issue to those around them. Information therefore flows from the project via the opinion leader to the recipient. This is also called the two-step flow model (Katz & Lazarsfeld, 1955). The opinion leader must be someone whom other stakeholders find it worthwhile listening to. This means that for a person to be an influential opinion leader, they must be attractive and credible. Credibility is often achieved through expertise and objectivity. For the opinion leader to have expertise, the relevant connection to the issue is an interest in it. Opinion leaders are generally most effective in communicating with stakeholders who already experience a need for information about the topic (Sweeney et al., 2008), because otherwise the stakeholders would not find it relevant to communicate about the issue with the opinion leader.

You need to be aware of stakeholders who are suitable to be opinion leaders, and you need to nurture them to be so. Union representatives or experienced employees can be relevant opinion leaders in some projects. The same applies to representatives of interest organizations, e.g. a representative of a citizens' association. These persons are not role models, because they are not typical employees or citizens. They are expected to know more and to take care of the interests of other stakeholders, and therefore they meet several of the criteria for having influence as opinion leaders.

## Where should the communication take place?

It is not enough to know what you want to say and how to say it. You also need to figure out *how to reach* your stakeholders. There are several alternatives for doing so, each with advantages and disadvantages.

An important decision concerns whether the communication will be *personal* or *impersonal*. Personal communication is one-to-one or one-to-few from the project manager, another spokesperson, or an opinion leader directly to the individual stakeholder. Impersonal communication is also called mass communication. In mass communication, which is one-to-many, the communicator is not necessarily a specific person; it can be, for example, a firm or the state. The recipient is not necessarily a specific person either; it can be, for example, a customer segment or all employees. On social media, communication can be one-to-one but is often many-to-many because everyone can contribute and see the contributions of others.

Another decision concerns whether the communication will be distributed as push or as pull communication. *Push communication* reaches recipients whether they want it or not. *Pull communication*, on the other hand, is made available to stakeholders who seek it out, e.g. citizens who are interested in following the progress of the construction of a new hospital. Figure 9.2 provides some examples of different types of push and pull communication that are often used with stakeholders, either personally or as mass communication.

In the following section, we will first review different forms of personal communication. Then we will look at mass communication.

| | Personal | Impersonal/mass |
|---|---|---|
| Push | Presentations at meetings on general issues<br>Workshops | Newsletters<br>Posters<br>Direct (e)mailing<br>Merchandise<br>Paid social media content |
| Pull | Online or in-person meetings about the issue<br>Hotline<br>Open-door policy | Social media content that the stakeholder subscribes to, such as a local area<br>Public or restricted project websites with databases, information, e-learning resources, etc. |

*Figure 9.2* Examples of different forms of communication

Along the way, we will include social media where relevant, and we will consider *media richness*, which is defined on four dimensions: (1) the possibility of feedback; (2) the number of stimuli that can be used (words, numbers, symbols); (3) linguistic variation (body, verbal, numbers); and (4) personal focus (Daft & Lengel, 1983; Daft et al., 1987). Media richness is important for the possibility to discuss issues with the stakeholders, as this requires the possibility to give personal feedback and the ability to convey complex information requiring different types of stimuli and linguistic variation to explain different elements and target stakeholders with different learning styles.

*Personal communication* can be both *push* and *pull*, because it can reach recipients who have not sought out information, and be used to answer a request for information from a stakeholder. Personal communication is *rich*. It allows communication to go both ways and between several persons at the same time; it is flexible and allows adjustment along the way. Personal communication thus provides good opportunities to express emotions. Face-to-face communication between two people is the richest form of communication. Online meetings is a leaner form of communication – how lean depends on whether the camera is turned on. Communication via the telephone is leaner, and pure written communication, e.g. in a memo, is very lean.

Because of its richness, personal communication is a good way to ensure a common understanding. A good result requires that you manage the conversation in a way that is effective in relation to the issues being discussed, and that you ensure that someone takes minutes along the way. A *meeting with relatively few participants* can be a good setting for personal communication. If you can manage the meeting in a good way, each participant can have important issues clarified, and you can tailor your answers so that you maximize the individual participant's understanding. It is a great advantage that communication can be adapted on the spot. For example, a stakeholder who fails to understand what is being said can ask for further explanation. It is also beneficial that tone of voice and body language can reveal uncertainty or anxiety. This informs you about when you need to signal openness to dialogue. These things mean that *concerns* that are big enough to create uncertainty or confusion, but not big enough to justify actual complaints, have a good chance of *being aired* and thus dealt with before they become problems.

You can also use *social media* for personal communication with stakeholders. Social media can facilitate conversations, e.g. about opinions on an action. But remember that the conversation on social media is not only between you and the stakeholder. The conversation can also be direct between stakeholders, and they may eagerly share their opinions. Therefore, a lot of communication, which you need to respond to, can quickly accumulate (Chung et al., 2023; Jepsen et al., 2025).

*Personal communication* also has *disadvantages.* It is more demanding than mass communication because the persons involved must meet at a given time and place. It can also be mentally demanding to participate in personal communication because it requires commitment from all parties for something fruitful to come out of the conversation.

The disadvantages of personal communication mean that *you should use it with caution.* Consider before you set out to convene a meeting that an uncommitted stakeholder is unlikely to be willing to spend time or other resources to attend. Conducting *meetings online saves resources for everyone* because no one must physically travel to a meeting location.

*Mass communication* is *impersonal communication.* Mass communication can be implemented in different ways. It can be implemented as *push communication* in the form of advertising or PR (public relations), or as *pull communication* by making information available in different ways. Mass communication is not required to be the same for all stakeholders. It can be adapted to stakeholder groups with different needs. Mass communication can be spread virtually over the internet or via radio, TV, or in the cinema. It can also be spread in print, e.g. on posters and leaflets. Another option is information meetings, which is mass communication if there are many participants, and the communication therefore becomes one-way. Social media has provided new opportunities for mass communication to stakeholders as paid advertising that can be targeted very precisely, and on own accounts where the project can spread communication to those who are interested in following the project.

*Advertising* can be placed on posters, flyers, over loudspeakers, and via paid content on various media. Advertising can also be placed on merchandise such as mugs and T-shirts with the project logo. It is important to be aware that merchandise only has value if the recipient appreciates it and uses it so that it is visible to others. This means that the merchandise must have good functionality for the target group, be suitable for public use, and fit the project. For example, unhealthy things such as candy are unfit as merchandise in connection with a project to improve food health.

You can also use *PR activities*. PR is publicity that the project does not pay for and that is not produced by the project team. PR is not free, because it costs the medium that hosts it resources to bring the communication. This means that it must have an interest in using space on doing so. To create this interest, you need to have a story to tell, which can be easily published, and which is of interest to the audience of the medium in question. Such a medium can be a company newsletter, for which you can create relevant content across the project course for such an outlet. In the early phases, the purpose of the project, and maybe who is involved, is relevant. Later, you can perhaps share experiences that employees who have been involved in development tasks in the project have had. In this way, you can use them as role models for other employees, who will provide input to the project. You may also use specialists associated with the project as opinion leaders. They can, for example, talk about expectations for the product that the project will develop. To support PR throughout the course of the project, you should *prepare how to mention the activities in connection with the project's milestones* when planning the project's timeline. Not least for megaprojects such as large infrastructure projects, you can benefit from creating a coherent story about the project, also called a narrative (Ninan & Sergeeva, 2022).

Mass communication that is pushed out to the stakeholders is *good at informing uninvolved stakeholders* because it does not require the stakeholder to actively seek out the information. Mass communication is good at creating awareness and thereby potential interest in the project, its deliverables, and results. It is economically efficient, and it can be prepared when it fits into the planning. It does not require a special relationship with the project and can therefore be prepared by, for example, the marketing department or an outside agency. Unfortunately, *mass communication only influences stakeholders to a limited extent* because the message, means, and timing are not adapted to personal characteristics and motivational factors. It is also uncertain if the communication will reach the stakeholders exactly when they need it. This means that the communication may be ignored and not perceived at all.

Mass communication requires *choosing which medium or channel* will carry the communication out to the stakeholders (the masses).

You should choose the channel based on a mapping of where the stakeholders go and which mass media and social media they typically use. This could be *print*, in the form of newspapers and magazines, *auditive media*, in the form of podcasts, or *visual media*, in the form of streaming services. If the project is large and has a large budget, you can use a marketing agency to help with this decision. If your project is small and possibly within your own organization, you will have to take other paths to reach your stakeholders. Then you can place the communication where the stakeholders are most likely to stumble upon it. This could, for example, be in the canteen, where people are queuing and waiting for service, it could be in hallways or on the company intranet, or at company meetings with other information sharing.

The stakeholder's level of involvement decides which channel is the best. Communication directly with stakeholders via email ensures that they will receive the communication. However, you have no guarantee that they will read your message. Some stakeholders may even be annoyed by being contacted personally and feel that you are spamming them. Therefore, it can be wiser to use media where you are less sure of reaching the stakeholder, but where there is also less risk that the stakeholder will feel personally offended by the communication.

Push mass communication is *ineffective in changing a negative attitude or in persuading a stakeholder to contribute if they do not intend to do so.* This is because it fails to consider the specific resistance and concerns of the stakeholder. Mass communication, on the other hand, is *well suited* to making marginal stakeholders aware of the project and *keeping them informed* throughout the project. It can also be well chosen for key players, resourcefuls, and showstoppers in those phases of the project when they have little interest in it. A potential user of a product under development may not be able to provide much useful information to a development project, and is therefore classified as a positive marginal, and he will not receive information about the project while it is running. This is probably wrong, as the potential user should ideally become an actual user after the project is completed, when the product is marketed. Therefore, the user is a resourceful who can generate value for the base organization by purchasing the product. Potential users will be more likely to buy the product when it is launched if they have been aware that it was under development. Then they may have imagined how they will buy and use it when it comes to the market. This is, for example, what happens when potential users are offered to test beta versions of software. The project should attract and maintain user attention through mass communication, e.g. on social media aimed at prospective users.

Impersonal *pull* communication is a good supplement to push mass communication and personal communication. There are many examples of pull communication. For example, some information may be stored in a database, while other information may be made available in an instructional video. Games and quizzes are also something that stakeholders actively access. Games can be used to teach stakeholders how to perform a task. Quizzes can be used to let stakeholders check their own learning in an entertaining way (Ingvarsson et al., 2023). Before choosing to use games and quizzes, you should consider whether it is suitable for the project topic and the target group. If not, you risk being perceived as frivolous.

You can make your pull communication available to a limited group of stakeholders, or to a large, unlimited audience on a website. You can also combine limited and unlimited access, so that some web pages are open to everyone, while others require a password. Pull communication can, for example, be made available on the internet, via a learning management system (LMS), or in a knowledge bank. Artificial intelligence (AI) offers good opportunities to give stakeholders the right information without them having to spend a lot of time searching for it themselves, e.g. by using a chatbot that you have constructed for this project. If you use generative AI, such as ChatGPT, Copilot, or Gemini, your chatbot can do more than just pass on information. It can combine creatively and thus create communication that suits what stakeholders are demanding. Generative AI learns through use and over time, because it can analyse the interactions it has. Therefore, it can improve during the project. Researchers believe that generative AI has great potential to revolutionize how project managers interact with stakeholders (e.g. Ahmed et al., 2024; Felicetti et al., 2024; Schindler, 2023).

Impersonal pull communication has many of the *same positive characteristics as push mass communication*, but not as many of the negative characteristics. It allows for efficient and planned development and publication of information, it is flexible, and it allows the use of many different types of stimuli: text, sound, and images. Finally, it can be the same for everyone but also allows for adaptation to the individual stakeholder. Therefore, impersonal pull communication can be *a good complement to personal communication*, e.g. as a resource to prepare for meetings and workshops and to follow up on issues that have come up in meetings and workshops.

You cannot reach all relevant stakeholders using pull communication, because stakeholders must actively seek out information provided this way. This *requires a certain level of interest* in the project. In addition, the stakeholder must be *aware* that the *information is available*, where it can be found, and have *access to the necessary technology* to make use of the resources you provide. All of this means that *pull communication cannot stand alone*; it must be complemented by communication that creates awareness of the project and informs stakeholders about the information available. You also need to consider how ambitious you want to be in your pull communication. It can range from a simple project page on a website to sophisticated database systems and e-learning platforms. The more advanced forms can be quite expensive to work with and are therefore best suited to communication that is relevant to many stakeholders.

In most projects, there is a need to bring *multiple distribution methods* into play to reach all types of stakeholders, and you can work to create synergy between the types of media that you use. Concerning stakeholders who are uninvolved in the project, you should first communicate with them to heighten their involvement. Once this is in place, you can communicate with them in ways that are better suited to influencing their attitude, such as detailed information about the project. This means that you should first use communication methods that are suitable for creating awareness, such as advertising or PR. You can perhaps use personal communication later. You can also reach more persons with the information you send out as mass communication by supporting personal communication between stakeholders, e.g. from opinion leaders to other stakeholders, as discussed earlier in this chapter. You can also use hashtags and links on social media, and you can make it easy to share your posts. You should carefully plan such a communication flow. Box 9.2 summarizes the choices you need to make for how to reach your stakeholders.

**Box 9.2 Choosing where the communication/ dissemination should take place**

- How can you create awareness of the project and its issues?
- Which stakeholders can you communicate with as a group/ mass?
- Which stakeholders or issues need personalized communication?
- Is there a need for a rich medium, or a can a lean medium be used?
- Will a given group of stakeholder(s) be interested in seeking out information themselves (push or pull)?
- How can PR support the project (the good story)?

## When and how often

Once you have decided how you will formulate your communication, who will present it, what means you will use to influence stakeholders, and how you will reach them, you need to decide when the communication should take place. The *timing* of the communication effort is determined by an analysis of (1) when *each stakeholder needs information or attention*, and (2) when *you need to communicate* with stakeholders to obtain information about their knowledge, expectations, or preferences or to provide stakeholders with necessary information. You can base the analysis of these issues on the results of your stakeholder analysis, which informs you about the communication tasks and needs that exist in the project phases.

Communication with stakeholders can be *synchronous*, meaning that the communication is sent and received at the same time. It can also be *asynchronous*, meaning that sending and receiving are separated in time (Carmel & Agarwal, 2001). The *advantage of using asynchronous* communication is that the communication can be prepared and delivered to many stakeholders at a time, which is independent from the time when the stakeholders need to receive the information. This means that you can do this work when it fits into your calendar. Asynchronous communication is therefore good for communication that needs to be available to the stakeholder when the stakeholder needs it, and when there is no need for someone to be ready to help the stakeholder when the stakeholder seeks information. The *disadvantage* of using asynchronous communication is that the project information may be made available at a time when the stakeholders are not interested in it. This means that they may ignore it or even feel that they are being spammed at one time, and at another time they experience that they are not told anything at all about what is happening. Asynchronous communication is also not very effective for decision-making processes that involve many parties or are complex because there is time between questions and answers. This means that communication can easily become very complicated, as you probably know from email discussions involving several people.

Because of these disadvantages, it can be more efficient to use *synchronous* communication, although it can be complicated. Synchronous communication requires that the participants in the communication are available at the same time and that someone spends time arranging a meeting. However, this work has been made easier in recent years because of sufficient bandwidth and good tools for conducting meetings online which has increased the possibility of using synchronous, rich communication media without needing to be physically present in the same place.

It can be useful to think about the tasks that need to be solved in *the different phases* of the project when planning the communication efforts over time, because different stakeholders and different issues are important in the different phases. In the *initiation phase* of the project, you are involved in complex negotiations with the stakeholders who are involved in decisions about the purpose and scope of the project. It is a process that requires synchronous communication that allows for flexibility and dialogue. This can, for example, take place in a workshop. If the project is geographically dispersed, you can choose to organize the workshop in a virtual space. An online workshop works best if the stakeholders are familiar with each other in advance and have a certain level of mutual trust. You can help stakeholders prepare for a workshop through mass communication, e.g. in the form of pre-distributed, written meeting documents. You can also consider creating a website where stakeholders can find relevant information along the way. It can be documents that describe the project, or simulation tools that can show the consequences of the project, e.g. how much noise there will be when a new airport is completed (Jepsen et al., 2025).

In the *planning phase*, you need to align expectations between stakeholders, create awareness about the project and its overall purpose, and start building relationships with stakeholders. Mass communication is good for creating awareness and aligning expectations among marginal stakeholders because this only requires that they receive the communication. Mass communication can also be useful to show positive resourcefuls how they can contribute in the way that is easiest for them, e.g. in video format. You need personal communication if you are going to form relationships or try to change a stakeholder's negative attitude, as mass communication is not particularly suitable for persuasion.

In the *implementation phase*, the focus is on keeping positive stakeholders informed and acknowledging the contributions they make to the project, and you need to maintain the relationships that have been built. For that, you again need both personal and impersonal communication. The same applies in the *closing phase*.

You need to plan the *intensity of communication* and the *organizational level* at which communication will take place across the project phases. There are times when more communication is needed, and perhaps at a higher organizational level, than during other, quieter periods. One reason for an increased need for communication may be that new, important stakeholders need to be involved in the project. Another reason may be that there is a crisis in the project. To be prepared for this, you can prepare a *crisis communication plan*, describing how communication intensity will be increased in certain situations with more frequent communication or by using richer media, e.g. moving from email to online meetings. You can also make use of your issue escalation plan, which we discussed in Chapter 8. Box 9.3 provides an overview of the timing considerations.

**Box 9.3 Timing considerations**

- What information do stakeholders need across the project phases?
- What information can be communicated asynchronously (cheaper), and what requires synchronous communication (more expensive)?

- Is it possible to use digital media to make synchronous communication cheaper?
- How should the intensity of communication be across the project phases?
- Are there topics or phases that require communication at a higher organizational level than others?
- What should happen in the event of a crisis?

## Put yourself in the shoes of the communication recipient

Planning your communication efforts requires that you decide what, who, how, where, and when to communicate about the project to and with the stakeholders, individually or as one or several groups. When you decide what to do, it's important to keep in mind that stakeholders have much less information about the project than you do. In many cases, the stakeholders are also much less committed to the project than you. Therefore, a mantra in communication efforts is to adapt your communication to the stakeholders' characteristics and needs and, in general, to make the communication as simple as possible.

As an example, we again take a closer look at the union representative from Tables 6.2 and 8.3. The union representative is involved in the project and can therefore be expected to allocate resources to receiving communication and give feedback to the project. Furthermore, the union representative can be classified as well-informed, wherefore he can understand and interpret relatively advanced information. The union representative needs ongoing information about project progress. This can be given in a newsletter on project progress. Furthermore, the union representative has been assigned at role in a reference group. He will need information to be able to prepare for meetings in a fair way. Such information can be given in a common workspace on SharePoint. Newsletters and meetings in the reference group are planned for major milestones in the project. Information materials for meetings in the reference group must be in place at least a week prior to a meeting.

**Mini-case 9 Equip all project participants for communication**

An engineering consulting company was given a sensitive project assignment by a customer. The customer needed to determine whether there was still contamination on a previously contaminated site, where the customer had just built an apartment complex with owner-occupied apartments.

The customer's concern was that even if the samples showed that there was no contamination, the mere suspicion that there might be contamination would create unrest among the people who had bought and now inhabited the apartments. The project manager from the engineering consulting firm was therefore tasked with carrying out the tests very discreetly – and prevent the press from getting wind of the examinations.

When the project was initiated, the consulting firm sent out a technician to take soil samples on the property. During the technician's work on this, a neighbour came over to hear what was going on. The technician, who had not heard that the samples were to be taken discreetly, thought that the friendly man deserved an answer, and readily told him that he was taking samples to check for contamination.

This conversation created rumours and concerns in the neighbourhood, which then reached the customer's ears. This led to a need for crisis management in the engineering consulting firm.

Source: Interview conducted by the authors. The case is anonymized

*The case illustrates that a project can get into problems if it fails to inform relevant stakeholders about why the project is going on in the area – in this case that samples are taken to be absolutely sure that there is no contamination, not because of an expectation to find contamination.*

*The case further illustrates that all project participants may engage with stakeholders, even if this is outside their role in the project. Therefore, decisions on how to communicate with stakeholders must be disseminated to all relevant project participants for them to have the desired effect.*

*The case finally illustrates that it is not enough to make general decisions about communication. You need to consider who might pass on information and what information they should pass on. In this case, the project participant who communicated with the neighbour was a person who was not used to or equipped for the task. For example, the technician didn't know the context in which the examinations were conducted; he just knew what tests to take.*

## References

Ahmed, M. S., Jannat, S. F., & Tanim, S. H. (2024). Artificial intelligence in public project management: Boosting economic outcomes through technological innovation. *International Journal of Applied Engineering & Technology*, 6 (4), 47–63.

Carmel, E., & Agarwal, R. (2001). Tactical approaches for alleviating distance in global software development. *IEEE Software*, 18 (2), 22–29.

Chung, K. S. K., Eskerod, P., Jepsen, A. L., & Zhang, J. (2023). Response strategies for community stakeholder engagement on social media: A case study of a large infrastructure project. *International Journal of Project Management*, 41 (5), 102495.

Daft, R. L., & Lengel, R. H. (1983). *Information richness. A new approach to managerial behavior and organization design*. DTIC Document.

Daft, R. L., Lengel, R. H., & Trevino, L. K. (1987). Message equivocality, media selection, and manager performance: Implications for information systems. *MIS Quarterly*, 11, 355–366.

Eisend, M. (2007). Understanding two-sided persuasion: An empirical assessment of theoretical approaches. *Psychology & Marketing*, 24 (7), 615–640.

Eskerod, P., & Jepsen, A. L. (2016). *Project stakeholder management*. Routledge.

Felicetti, A. M., Cimino, A., Mazzoleni, A., & Ammirato, S. (2024). Artificial intelligence and project management: An empirical investigation on the appropriation of generative Chatbots by project managers. *Journal of Innovation & Knowledge*, 9 (3), 100545.

Ingvarsson, C., Hallin, A., & Kier, C. (2023). Project stakeholder engagement through gamification: What do we know and where do we go from here? *International Journal of Managing Projects in Business*, 16 (8), 152–181.

Jepsen, A. L., Eskerod, P., Chung, K. S. K., Zhang, J., & Ortiz, M. (2025). Using websites and social media to support local community stakeholder attendance at project town hall meetings. *Project Leadership & Society*, 6, 100164.

Katz, E., & Lazarsfeld, P. F. (1955). *Personal influence, the part played by people in the flow of mass communications.* The Free Press.

McElroy, B., & Mills, C. (2003). Managing stakeholders. In R. J. Turner (Ed.), *People in project management* (pp. 99–118). Gower.

Ninan, J., & Sergeeva, N. (2022). Battle of narratives: Interaction between narratives and counter-narratives in megaprojects. *Project Leadership and Society*, 3, 100069.

Ohanian, R. (1990). Construction and validation of a scale to measure celebrity endorsers' perceived expertise, trustworthiness, and attractiveness. *Journal of Advertising*, 19 (3), 39–52.

Pavlov, I. P. (1927). *Conditioned reflexes: An investigation of the physiological activity of the cerebral cortex.* Oxford University Press.

Petty, R. E., Cacioppo, J. T., & Schumann, D. (1983). Central and peripheral routes to advertising effectiveness: The moderating role of involvement. *Journal of Consumer Research*, 10 (2), 135.

Schindler, P. (2023). *Successful project management with AI: Boost productivity in traditional and agile projects.* Springer Nature.

Skinner, B. F. (1938). *The behavior of organisms: An experimental analysis.* Appleton-Century.

Sweeney, J. C., Soutar, G. N., & Mazzarol, T. (2008). Factors influencing word of mouth effectiveness: Receiver perspectives. *European Journal of Marketing*, 42 (3/4), 344–364.

# 10 The engagement plan

You and your project owner make many decisions about the project stakeholder engagement. We recommend that you document and keep these decisions in an engagement plan. The engagement plan comprises an *overall plan* and an *action plan*. Below, we elaborate on the two plans.

## The overall plan

The overall part of the engagement plan contains the overall decisions on stakeholder engagement in the project, a follow-up plan, a crisis communication plan, shared communication materials, and other general items for project stakeholder engagement.

The *overall decisions* on stakeholder engagement comprise how to communicate the *project's purpose, scope, and plan* as well as the *project's overall message*. They also concern *guidelines for collaboration and communication*, such as requirements for diversity, i.e. representation of different types of stakeholders, and a possible delegation of the *responsibility* for planning and following up on the stakeholder engagement.

The *follow-up plan* can be tied to dates for milestones, deliverables, or project phases. There is no general rule for when and how it is most appropriate to follow up on the stakeholder engagement plan. This depends on the circumstances and situation of the specific project, but it is good practice to review the stakeholder register and the action plan at transitions between project phases and in connection with major decisions in the project. In addition, you can ensure ongoing follow-up by making evaluation of the stakeholder engagement efforts a permanent item on the agenda of project status meetings.

DOI: 10.4324/9781003712695-10

The follow-up process should evaluate *the effect of the actions* that have been made to ensure the necessary contributions. An insightful evaluation is only possible if the engagement plan contains precise, operational objectives. Unfortunately, it is not possible to define all the objectives so that they can be followed up on in a simple way. There are many soft objectives in stakeholder engagement, such as changing a stakeholder attitude towards a given issue. A further challenge in the evaluation is that it can be difficult to collect the relevant data without the stakeholders feeling that they are burdened by an endless number of evaluations. Therefore, it may be difficult to obtain the necessary data from the stakeholders. Instead, you can use data that do not involve the stakeholder directly, e.g. the number of inquiries about problems by phone, email, or in person, and perhaps development in number of inquiries. Sometimes it is possible to use data from the project plan and controlling, for example, whether a supplier delivers on time.

During follow-up, you should also assess whether *new stakeholders have emerged*, if *new stakeholder information has emerged*, and if any of the stakeholders have *changed attitude, potential to influence positively or negatively*, or how they perceive to be *influenced by the project*. If new stakeholders have emerged, you should analyse them in the same way that you have previously analysed other stakeholders. Be aware that new stakeholders may lack knowledge about the project and the stakeholder engagement that has taken place before they came along. You should follow up on the emergence of new stakeholders as a regular part of the general follow-up on the engagement plan, but you can add new stakeholders to your stakeholder register at any time when you become aware of them. This also applies if you become aware that you have overlooked a stakeholder in the original stakeholder analysis.

The overall plan also comprises *communication materials* that can be used across different groups of stakeholders, such as graphic design, e.g. a logo or an illustration, and information on the project's purpose and plan. Such material should be accessible to everyone who works with stakeholders.

It can be beneficial to include a *list of definitions* of key terms, such as project deliverables, milestones, and relevant technical and regulatory terms. Such a list helps ensure that communication about the project is consistent and unambiguous.

Finally, the crisis communication plan with issue escalation plan is part of the overall plan.

Box 10.1 lists the main elements of the overall plan for stakeholder engagement.

**Box 10.1 The overall plan for stakeholder engagement**

- Decisions on how to communicate project purpose, scope, and plan
- Guidelines for engagement and communication with stakeholders
- Follow-up plan for the stakeholder register and action plan
- Delegation of responsibility
- Communication material
- List of definitions
- Crisis communication plan with issue escalation plan

## The action plan

The action plan is based on the results of the stakeholder analysis and the decisions made on engagement of each (group of) stakeholder(s). Table 10.1 (and Appendix C) shows an action plan. The plan must be completed as follows:

1 Copy stakeholders with category and challenges and opportunities from the stakeholder register (Table 6.2). Challenges and opportunities can be supplemented by additional information on communication issues.
2 Decide strategy, engagement tactics, and actions (Table 8.2) based on (1).
3 Decide communication based on decisions in (2). Use Figures 9.1 and 9.2, Tables 9.1–9.3, and Boxes 9.1 and 9.2.
4 Plan when the actions will take place. Use the timing considerations (Box 9.3).
5 Who is responsible for each stakeholder? This person is responsible for following up on planned activities. We recommend that each stakeholder has one contact person in the project organization, so that the stakeholder always knows who to turn to if there are any questions.

*Table 10.1* Action plan for stakeholder engagement example

| *Stakeholder with category* | *Challenges and opportunities* | *Strategy* | *Engagement tactics* | *Planned actions* | *Communication* | *When* | *Responsible* |
|---|---|---|---|---|---|---|---|
| Project owner – positive key player | May lose interest as the project progresses | Maintain the stakeholder in the current state | Support the perception of fairness | Communicate progress and results | Dialogue and visual aids | At project status meetings | Project manager |
| Union representative – key player (neither positive nor negative) | Can be challenged by negative employees | Maintain the stakeholder in the current state | Support the perception of contributing<br>Support the perception of fairness | Inform on an ongoing basis<br>Assign formal role in the project: member of reference group | Newsletter<br>Participation in meetings<br>Access to project information on SharePoint | At major milestones<br>Meeting materials ready one week before meeting | Project manager |
| Negative employees – marginals, but as group key player | May be worried if their skills suffice with the new work tasks<br>Can team up with other negative members | Influence attitude in a positive direction or overcome the negative attitude | Change the expectation of how the new action influences the work processes | Inform about consequences<br>Include stakeholder proposals in planning | Information, possibly visualization of workflow using role models<br>Presented at a meeting and made available online after the meeting | At the start of the project | Julian Smith (team member) |

Notes: Dark grey=high need for attention, light grey=some need for attention, white=no need for attention now

To support your understanding, we have completed the action plan in Table 10.1 with the same stakeholders of the change project, which we showed in Tables 6.2 and 8.3. We have copied the first two columns from the stakeholder register in Table 6.2, and the next three columns from Table 8.3. We have added decisions on communication, when the actions are to take place, and who is responsible. We again look closer at the union representative, who is involved in the project, and therefore who can be expected to allocate resources to receiving communication and give feedback to the project. The union representative is a key player in need of some attention (light grey). He needs ongoing information on project progress, which can be given in a newsletter. The union representative has been assigned a role in a reference group, and he needs special information to prepare for meetings. Such information can be given in a common workspace, e.g. on SharePoint. The information must be given at important milestones in the project. To show respect for the role as union representative, the project manager keeps the responsibility for the contact with the union representative instead of delegating it.

## The plan is dynamic

So far, we have focused on how you can create an overview of the project's stakeholders and plan your engagement from a static perspective. We have talked about *the* stakeholder analysis, *the* stakeholder register, and *the* engagement plan. But the world is dynamic, and therefore the assumptions behind the plans are constantly changing, and more knowledge constantly added.

The *initial planning* of stakeholder engagement should take place during the project initiation phase to ensure that key stakeholders are engaged from the beginning. You should already at this point be ensuring that resources are allocated for stakeholder engagement, and that you agree with your project owner on how much effort should be put into the engagement.

*How detailed* the engagement plan needs to be at various stages in the project depends on the *characteristics of the project* and *how flexible the project is planned*. If the project is a delivery project, such as a construction project, and it is a type of project that the organization has experience in implementing, you may be able to decide and plan the project in detail from the start. If, on the other hand, the project is a development project, where the final deliverable is unclear and the methods to be used during the project are also unclear, the project is typically planned in a more flexible way, e.g. agile. The engagement plan must reflect this situation and be developed continuously as the project progresses.

It is *dangerous to rely on the initial action plan* throughout the project because early in the project you lack information to characterize the stakeholders and assess who is more or less important. Therefore, you need to do detailed analysis of the stakeholders and engagement planning in the planning phase of the project, and you will most likely need to do several revisions in connection with your follow-up activities. Revisions can be made in a copy of the original plan, which is updated according to the current situation. We suggest that you keep a log of the changes you make.

In our research, we have seen many challenges in working with project stakeholders, even though time and resources were spent on planning stakeholder engagement. Often, this was due to changes in the stakeholder composition or in the stakeholders' knowledge and/or attitudes that had not been included in the engagement plan along the way. Perhaps the stakeholders were not fully aware of their own preferences early in the project. Perhaps they felt that they didn't know the project manager and the team well enough to reveal their thoughts and concerns to them. Perhaps they did so later in the project.

Failure to update the engagement plan can result in too much time being spent on stakeholders who have lost importance and too little on stakeholders who have gained importance and thus need more attention than originally planned. Lack of attention can result in issues being allowed to grow unnoticed, or stakeholders ceasing to engage with the project because they feel overlooked, forgotten, or perhaps even treated unfairly. You must ensure that what you learn is included in the revision of the engagement plan that occurs during the ongoing follow-up, and you may well need to repeat the analyses as new stakeholders emerge and knowledge and understanding of the stakeholders grow and reveal new issues.

**Mini-case 10 Four-day working week**

A survey shows that four out of five academics want a shorter working week – and preferably in a model where their working week consists of fewer hours without a salary reduction. In 2023, about 60 Danish companies followed this model. In 2025, this number had grown to more than 200, which is a 333% increase. The growth will most likely continue, as there is great interest in this model from several companies and public workplaces.

The firm PanzerGlass is headquartered in Denmark. It has subsidiaries and a presence in many countries. In 2022, PanzerGlass initiated a global project to implement a four-day working week throughout the company. The project resulted in the company deciding that the working week would, in the future, be four days. The length of each day would be the same as before. As a starting point, most employees would be given Friday off every second week. The salary was maintained as before. With this decision, PanzerGlass wanted to create a good work–life balance for its employees. The company also wanted to maintain and improve its ability to attract future talent.

The decision was to be implemented through a project, which was carried out with the help of an external consultant from the consulting firm Take Back Time. The consultant assisted with advice, sparring, and perspectives – and with a network that could supply contacts to companies and people with whom the project team could meet and receive input.

The employees at PanzerGlass express great satisfaction with the result of the project. In 2024, 96% of the respondents in a survey conducted by the global certification organization Great Place to Work answered that PanzerGlass is a good place to work. PanzerGlass sees the result of the project, i.e. the four-day working week, as part of a larger transformation of the workplace. The firm has implemented several additional initiatives, one at a time, e.g. by encouraging limiting meetings to 25 or 50 minutes instead of 30 or 60 minutes, so that there is time for breaks.

Sources: Arnedal (2021), PanzerGlass (2025), Santesson (2023), and Take Back Time (2025)

*The case illustrates that a project can expand its network and add expertise to the project by using a consulting firm. On top of expertise, the consulting firm may have experience across industries. The consulting firm may also have built a network that it can draw on and that it can share with the project. This gives the project access to resourcefuls who can provide inspiration and sparring and perhaps even participate as role models or opinion leaders.*

*By following a desire that is significant in society, in this case a four-day working week, the base organization, PanzerGlass, seeks to make itself attractive to talented future job applicants through the results of a change project. Thus, both current and potential future employees are stakeholders in the project.*

*The case draws our attention to the fact that the end of a project is not necessarily a final destination for the base organization. More value can be created from the project by implementing more actions in the base organization afterwards.*

*The case points out that the value of a project for the members of the base organization can, for example, be measured by externally conducted employee satisfaction surveys.*

## References

Arnedal, P. (2021). *Pernille har en mission: Et lykkeligt arbejdsliv og en 4-dages arbejdsuge* [Pernille has a mission: A happy work life and a 4-day workweek]. Web article published 23 November. https://pov.international/et-lykkeligt-arbejdsliv-og-en-4-dages-arbejdsuge/.

PanzerGlass (2025). *4-day workweek.* https://careers.panzerglass.com/pages/4-day-workweek. Accessed 13 August 2025.

Santesson, T. (2023). *Sådan tager I snakken om en 4-dages-arbejdsuge* [How to talk about a 4-day workweek]. Web article published 18 April. https://www.djoefbladet.dk/artikler/2023/04/guide-saadan-tager-i-snakken-om-4-dages-uge.

Take Back Time (2025). *Vi skaber lykkelige medarbejdere og sunde virksomheder* [We create happy employees and healthy companies]. https://www.takebacktime.dk/. Accessed 13 August 2025.

# 11 Complex, but can be learnt

Project stakeholder engagement is a complex task. It can be difficult to identify stakeholders, and it can be difficult to obtain the necessary information about them. In addition, project stakeholders influence and are influenced by the project in different ways, and they often have conflicting interests that can be challenging to balance.

As a project manager, you must try to acquire the necessary information and plan your stakeholder engagement to accommodate the different interests. In this chapter, we present some ethical and other challenges that you may encounter on your journey, and we conclude with some general advice.

## Ethical challenges

Ethical challenges arise when you must balance what is best from the perspective of the project or your personal interest, and what is proper or correct behaviour. Ethical conduct in a project context is professional, responsible behaviour. When you act otherwise, we see the dark side of the project. This also applies to working with stakeholders.

Behaviour that can lead to the dark side can have a political, an intellectual, and a moral dimension (Locatelli et al., 2022). The *political* dimension concerns whether you consider and adapt to the context that you are in. For example, the same code of conduct does not apply in a bank and in a nursing home. Similarly, correct behaviour depends on the culture you are in, e.g. the appropriateness of weighing financial considerations in comparison with other issues, and what are regarded as suitable questions to ask. The *intellectual* dimension

DOI: 10.4324/9781003712695-11

concerns whether you reflect on your practices. It may well be that you, in your education, have learned to do things in a certain way. This may no longer be regarded as the proper way. An example of something that was considered the right approach in former times is the *managing of stakeholders* approach. In recent years, it has increasingly been replaced by a *managing for stakeholders* approach, because it is no longer considered proper behaviour to try to manage your stakeholders narrowly based on your own interests. The *moral* dimension concerns whether you can tell the difference between "right and wrong" and how you handle knowledge of illegal actions and other immoral behaviour. Table 11.1 provides an overview of the three dimensions with examples of challenges in stakeholder engagement linked to each dimension.

It can be a challenge if there is a *lack of consensus about whether the project is successful.* This challenge is political, because assessing whether the project is a success depends on the eyes that see. Narrowly speaking, a project is seen as successful if it stays within the project triangle and leads to the planned value creation in the base organization. This may conflict with the interests of other stakeholders and thus their perspective on project success. For example, an owner of a nursing home may see it as successful if an efficiency improvement

*Table 11.1* Elements of unethical conduct in stakeholder engagement

| *Dimension* | *What it concerns* | *Example* |
|---|---|---|
| Political | Lack of consideration for context | When gathering information, you fail to consider that the project takes place in a nursing home with many vulnerable residents |
| Intellectual | Lack of consideration of whether learned solution models are (still) correct | You have learned in your education to take on a project perspective. Therefore, you try to reach the best solution for the project without considering if this destroys values for stakeholders |
| Moral | Illegal and other morally wrong behaviour | You avoid interfering when you have become aware that someone is conducting an illegal action or other immoral behaviour |

Source: Based on Locatelli et al. (2022)

project leads to less time being spent distributing medicine to residents. But perhaps the efficiency improvement has come at the expense of the time that the staff has for resident contact. Therefore, both staff and residents may feel a loss of value, and the project is therefore not a success, seen from their perspectives.

The fact that projects *run for a limited time* presents an ethical challenge, mostly of an intellectual nature. You may be tempted to deal with stakeholders from a short-term perspective, where you only think about achieving success within the project triangle, and fail to consider the long-term effects of the project. With a short-term perspective, you may ignore certain stakeholders, or you may ignore negative side effects that will arise in the future and destroy value for stakeholders in the long term.

Another intellectual dark side that emerges from *focusing unilaterally on achieving success within the project triangle* is that you may ignore the impact that your actions could have on your relationships with stakeholders. You may end up pressuring some stakeholders unnecessarily to finish on time or to stay within budget. You should consider your success criteria so that you create as much value as possible for everyone. This means striving to create value for the base organization without causing a loss of value for any stakeholder. Ethical behaviour seeks to avoid destruction of value as described in Chapter 2 about the *least well-off stakeholder*. To prevent short-termism and too narrow a focus on the project triangle, we suggest that you discuss with the project owner how to incorporate long-term issues into the project's success indicators, if they are not already there.

Projects are based on *negotiations between the project manager and the stakeholders*. Negotiation can be done with a collaborative approach, a power-oriented approach, or a combination of the two. A purely power-oriented approach, where you use a powerful position to put pressure on one or more stakeholders, may seem very effective, but it is generally not in line with modern management principles. This is a challenge on the intellectual dimension. It is not ethically correct behaviour to force or manipulate stakeholders to adhere to your needs, not even if it is done to serve the interests of the base organization. A power-oriented approach is, however, not always unethical. It can be ethically correct if you believe that it is in the stakeholder's interest, but you lack means or time to convince the stakeholder about this. You may be pushing your solution through because you have greater insight into the current issue and the consequences of different alternatives than the stakeholder has. It may also be that time pressure means that immediate action is necessary and that there is therefore no time for a collaborative approach.

As a project manager, you typically have more detailed knowledge about the project than the project owner and others in the organization. *The level of information is asymmetric* (Akerlof, 1982). This presents a moral challenge. The asymmetric information is to your advantage because you can choose not to share important information with the project owner if, for example, the information casts the project or yourself in a bad light. For example, you may obtain information that threatens the existence of the project but which you would like to withhold because you want the project to continue. Perhaps you or someone on the project team finds out that a competitor is ready to market a product that will make the product that your team is developing redundant. With that knowledge, it would be better to stop the project immediately and transfer the resources to other activities and projects. However, if you and your team enjoy the technical challenges associated with developing the product, or if your team is only employed for the duration of the project, you may be tempted to postpone sharing the new knowledge as long as possible.

Throughout the book, we have encouraged you to gather knowledge and share information with others. However, this is not without challenges. There can be a moral challenge associated with *when to share information with others*. This could, for example, be about unexpected problems in the project. You should not burden those who decide whether the project should continue with all small problems that arise along the way. On the other hand, it is important that decision-makers receive information about problems that might influence their opinion about allocation of resources to the project. The challenging issue here is to balance the urge to cope with the problems within the project, and the need of the project owner and other decision-makers to be updated on any issues and potential challenges. As a project manager you should pay particular attention to this delicate balance.

Ethical challenges in information sharing are often complex because the *knowledge* that you gain may be *open to interpretation*. Perhaps information about a competitor's product development is based on hearsay, and its truth value may not be verifiable without drawing attention to your own project and its product development. It may also be unclear how powerful the competitor's new product really is. Therefore, it may be unclear when you have enough certain knowledge to pass it on.

A particular dilemma concerns *how to allocate your limited time among the different stakeholders.* This can be a moral and an intellectual challenge. Perhaps you must spend time on a powerful stakeholder. Another stakeholder may require attention because they have an urgent need for one or more of the project's deliverables. You may find yourself in a situation where you must decide who to spend time on – the powerful stakeholder or the person who needs the deliverable? There is no easy solution to this. It makes sense to spend time finding a good solution, because otherwise the project process may be perceived as unfair. This may deprive some stakeholders of the motivation to contribute to the project. A perception that the project process is unfair is especially problematic if the stakeholders are part of the same network and therefore share knowledge about experiences – good as well as bad.

Another issue is that stakeholder engagement involves *targeted behaviour to influence other persons.* According to the guidelines that we have presented in this book, you should plan your stakeholder engagement based on an analysis of when and how it is best to invest time and effort in building and maintaining a relationship with a given stakeholder. This means that you enter communication with stakeholders with a specific purpose in mind. The communication is planned in terms of time, extent, and content. This also applies to the conversations you have with the aim of uncovering expectations and wishes in relation to the project. This can be considered morally wrong because it can be seen as manipulation.

It is therefore best to be open about it if a meeting or conversation is happening with the purpose of generating information or otherwise advancing the project. On the other hand, it can be dangerous to be completely open about the agenda if the stakeholder is someone who can and will use that knowledge to their own advantage. This is especially true if the stakeholder is uncertain whether you will practise project management and stakeholder engagement in a fair way.

We have pointed out several times throughout the book that *stakeholders have their own stakeholders.* This raises two moral issues. The first is that you may put so much pressure on your stakeholders that it is difficult for them to consider their own stakeholders, such as their employees or suppliers. It is ethically wrong to take advantage of a skewed balance of power, so if you can exert pressure because the balance of power is skewed in your favour, you need to consider your actions.

The second issue arises if a stakeholder behaves in an ethically incorrect way towards their own stakeholders, for example by using child labour or underpaying employees. In that situation, you should consider whether you want to maintain the relationship with the stakeholder, try to get him or her to change behaviour, end the relationship, or perhaps even report your observations to relevant authorities.

Box 11.1 summarizes the ethical challenges we have discussed here.

### Box 11.1 Ethical challenges in stakeholder engagement

- Stakeholders and the project may have different perspectives on value and thus whether the project is a success
- When you create value for the base organization, you may destroy value for others
- A short-term perspective on optimizing the project may blind you to long-term consequences
- You may use your power to pressure stakeholders unnecessarily
- You may use the fact that you have more knowledge about the project than others to your own advantage
- It can be difficult to know when you are confident enough in your knowledge to share it
- It can be difficult to assess how to best allocate your limited time between stakeholders
- Stakeholders may perceive a very well-planned stakeholder engagement as manipulative
- You must take into account that stakeholders also have other relationships to consider than you and the project
- You may be challenged by immoral or illegal actions by stakeholders

## Other challenges

Ethical challenges are not the only challenges you may face in your stakeholder engagement. Some challenges arise because you will never be able to predict human behaviour with certainty. *Behaviour will always to some extent be unpredictable.* This is amplified in projects because some stakeholders may have relationships with each other that may be stronger than their relationship with the project. This means that *stakeholders can influence each other* in ways that may be difficult to predict.

It can also be a challenge to judge *how much analysis and planning of stakeholder engagement should take up compared to the time you spend with the stakeholders.* If you fail to spend time creating the necessary foundation for stakeholder engagement, you risk facing many challenges in your stakeholder engagement. On the other hand, if you spend too much time on analysis and planning, there is no time left to engage the stakeholders.

Your *personal resources for stakeholder engagement are limited.* Be careful not to spend more energy than you have on stakeholder engagement. There are an infinite number of things you can do in relation to stakeholders, so be careful not to overburden yourself with too-high ambitions. To keep the costs of time, effort, and money within reasonable limits, you should think about which stakeholders are sufficiently important for it to be reasonable to spend time gathering information about their expectations and concerns. It may be advantageous to at first only analyse the stakeholders that are important in the initiation phase and create a detailed stakeholder register with other stakeholders as they become important.

It is also a challenge to *get the necessary information from the stakeholders.* Stakeholders can only share information about their requirements, wishes, concerns, and preferences if they are aware of them. They must also be willing to share the information with the person asking. This challenge is enlarged by the fact that *a project is a temporary organization.* Therefore, both in the project and around it, there will be stakeholders with whom you have never had contact, and who have limited experience with the project's field. This may mean that important information about the stakeholders is challenging to acquire. To overcome this barrier, you must invest the necessary time and effort in building relationships with stakeholders to encourage them to share their considerations. Workshops, interviews, systemic constellations, and other forms of engagement can help stakeholders become aware of possible concerns and clarify their thoughts about the project. It can also help build a trusting relationship with the project manager and the team.

*Communication with the stakeholders* is also a challenge. It is complicated by differences in background and if the stakeholders are unfamiliar with each other, or the project manager, before the project starts. A common language in relation to the project topics may be lacking. Or there is no natural code of conduct – it is not established through the organizational culture, because the project organization is put together for the occasion. In addition, the base organization, the project, and the stakeholders may have different perceptions of value, and therefore there may be a lack of agreement on how to prioritize the project resources.

A further challenge in communication with and among stakeholders is that *stakeholders can be biased in their opinion of other stakeholders.* This can also apply within the project organization. Attitudes are often based on generalizations and stereotypes. For example, a designer may have an opinion about what engineers are like – and vice versa. In the worst case, this means that stakeholders fail to see the person behind the role and fail to listen to what others say and instead form their own distorted perception of what is being said and why, creating problems in mutual understanding and thus also in collaboration and problem-solving.

You can prevent communication challenges if, at the beginning of the project, you work at creating a common understanding of the project's purpose and goals and give your team the opportunity to create a code of conduct for stakeholder engagement.

## Ready for stakeholder engagement

Stakeholder engagement in projects is not characterized by clear cause-and-effect relationships and, therefore, there is no recipe or script for how to collaborate with your stakeholders in all situations. Unfortunately – or fortunately – the world is not that simple.

There are many challenges associated with analysing and planning project stakeholder engagement, but these activities can provide great value. They represent an ongoing learning process. They create opportunities to engage with stakeholders to learn about their thoughts and perceptions of the project at an early stage in the project's life cycle as well as throughout the project course. From a collaborative perspective on stakeholder engagement, we believe that stakeholder analysis and planning can contribute to your success as a project manager.

It is likely that you, your team members, and the stakeholders will meet again later, and some of you will have had contact with each other before. This all gives reason to work with stakeholders from a long-term perspective instead of focusing on optimizing the current project. With a long-term perspective, you focus on creating success for the project while also being aware of whether there are positive or negative side effects of the decisions you make in relation to current and future relationships with stakeholders.

A long-term perspective also means that it is not only tangible results that play a role; intangible and procedural results may be more important for future relationships than optimal delivery of all project deliverables.

Stakeholder analysis and planning should be repeated throughout the project life cycle. It is not a task that you accomplish in one attempt from behind a desk at the start of the project. When the plan can be in place varies greatly depending on the type of project. In some projects, it may be impossible or even destructive to settle on an engagement plan developed at an early stage. The engagement plan is a document based on interpretations of the stakeholders and the project made at a specific point in time. It is therefore not set in stone – and certainly not the universal truth.

We hope that the book, and the conceptual frameworks and tools that it contains, will help you in your work, not least by giving you increased awareness of your unspoken and perhaps unconscious ideas about stakeholders and how you best collaborate with them. We believe that increased reflection and dialogue within the project and between the project and its stakeholders will be to the benefit of all parties. An open mind allows you to capture stakeholders' requirements, wishes, concerns, and preferences throughout the project. On this basis, you can act in a way that supports stakeholders' necessary contributions while taking their interests into account.

We hope that the guidelines we have presented in this book will create a good framework for this to happen, and we believe that *stakeholder engagement is complex, but can be learned.*

**Mini-case 11 The project owner who lost interest**

A hospital went through a governmentally required accreditation process for continued operations and to maintain its status as an emergency hospital. To achieve the approval, several projects were initiated. One of the projects was for the preparation and implementation of a companywide guideline on resuscitation. With many patients, staff, and visitors in the hospital daily, it made sense that not just the staff at the emergency and intensive care units but the staff in general were trained in resuscitation.

The project made good progress during the accreditation process, but when the accreditation was in place, the hospital director lost interest in the project – and thought that the resources should be used elsewhere. This annoyed the project manager, who was passionate about the project, and who had received positive feedback about it from colleagues. She was unsure whether she should readily comply with her project owner and scale down the activities without questions – or if she should try to influence him to become more committed again, e.g. by pointing to the positive feedback from colleagues or by asking colleagues to attempt to influence him.

Source: Interviews conducted by the authors. The case is anonymized

*The case illustrates how a project manager can be divided between the interests of different stakeholders. The hospital director, who is the project owner, wants to shrink the project to enable use of the resources in other parts of the base organization, while another stakeholder group, namely the hospital staff, wants the project to be carried out to achieve the desired benefits in the form of rapid and professional resuscitation (as far as possible) of people who suffer cardiac arrest outside the emergency and intensive care units.*

*The project manager disagrees with a key player, the hospital director. The case thus illustrates that a stakeholder can have a different mindset than the project manager. The hospital director focuses on the accreditation authorities and not on the other, less powerful stakeholders, while the project manager focuses on the people in need.*

*The different perspectives entail disagreement on prioritization of the hospital's resources. The project manager finds that the interest of the people who are in focus in the project are such that resources should be allocated to the resuscitation project. However, from the hospital director's perspective, these people are not important compared to many other groups that have needs and the many other requirements, such as treatment guarantees, which the organization must also find resources to meet. He therefore finds that the resources should be spent otherwise.*

## References

Akerlof, G. A. (1982). Labor contracts as a partial gift exchange. *Quarterly Journal of Economics*, 97 (4), 543–569.

Locatelli, G., Konstantinou, E., Geraldi, J., & Sainati, T. (2022). The dark side of projects: Dimensionality, research methods, and agenda. *Project Management Journal*, 53 (4), 367–381.

# Cases

All cases are fictional.

## Case 1 Digitalization of customer contact in Easybuild

Easybuild is a house construction company whose main business is renovation projects for private homeowners. The company was founded in 1996 by Alice Smith. Two years ago, Alice started a generational change. Her children, Jan Smith and Anna Billinger, will both be transferred 10% of the shares every year, except for the last year, when Jan Smith will receive 11% and Anna Billinger 9%. Anna Billinger will be financially compensated for this difference. Right now, Alice Smith owns 60% of the shares, and each of the children 20%. Jan Smith is a certified public accountant and currently works for the global professional services firm, Deloitte. Anna Billinger is a trained pedagogue and works in a kindergarten, close to where she lives.

Easybuild has, in recent years, had an annual turnover of approximately €13 million, and a revenue of approximately €1.3 million per year. It has 75 employees. The management team consists of CEO Alice Smith, finance and IT manager Khalid Ourida, administration manager Peter Olsen, and construction and operations manager Piotr Patek. Alice Smith, Peter Olsen, and Piotr Patek are on the board of directors. The board also includes Jan Smith, Anna Billinger, and chairman of the board Oscar Olsen, who have extensive experience with board work. The departments under Piotr Patek employs a mix of skilled and unskilled workers. Each department has a foreman.

Alice Smith has, in agreement with her children, decided that Jan Smith will take over as CEO on 1 January the year after the coming

DOI: 10.4324/9781003712695-12

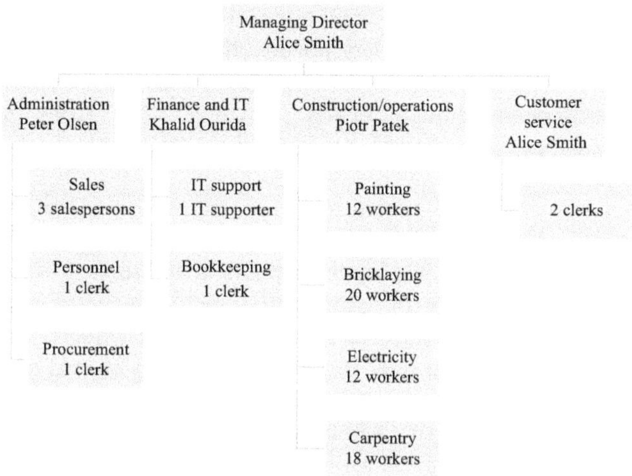


*Figure C.1* Easybuild organizational chart

year. At this point he will own 40% of the shares. He will start at Easybuild five months before taking over as CEO – on 1 August. There is a written agreement that Jan Smith at this point will start buying Anna Billinger's shares over a period of five years according to an agreed price schema that is attached to the net asset value of the company at the date of the purchase.

Since Alice Smith has known for some time that she will resign, the company's development has been stagnant for the past few years. Focus has been on working according to standard practice, which Alice Smith believes gives the best result. New ideas have not been welcome. The head of construction and operations, Piotr Patek, manages the construction in the same way, focusing on checking that things are being done correctly and on initiating corrective actions in case of problems. If problems arise on a construction site, the worker will contact the foreman, who will try to resolve the issue. If the foreman fails in this, they get in touch with Piotr Patek for further advice. It is not common practice for workers to turn to each other for help in these cases.

Jan Smith's takeover approaches. He is therefore increasingly eager to engage the company in development projects that will ensure long-term prosperity. At the same time, however, his sister, Anna Billinger, is against change. She points out possible risks of spending money on smart projects, as she calls them. She prefers a strategy that leads to slow growth or stability and believes that now is the wrong time to take risks. Anna Billinger and Jan Smith have an ongoing debate on this issue.

Lately, Jan Smith has started to investigate and assess various processes in Easybuild. He has become aware that customers often complain about details in the project proposals they are sent. They also complain about invoices for extra work done in connection with the work agreed in the contract for their renovation project. In their complaints, clients often refer to conversations they've had with various company representatives about the work they'd like to have done, about deviations along the way in the project process, and the extra payments that result. Jan Smith has inquired within Easybuild about this problem. The enquiries have confirmed that most of the communication with customers about renovation projects undertaken by the company is verbal, either in person or by telephone. It turns out that the foremen spend about 60% of their working time on follow-up in connection with changes in agreed renovation projects. Around 50% of this time is spent driving between customers.

Jan Smith is, through his job, used to working with various software and to focusing on documentation. He has also become quite adept at conducting online meetings. Inspired by this, Jan Smith has proposed to the board to take on a project for digitalizing meetings with customers. Jan Smith's reasoning for the project is that (1) the company will save on transportation costs, and (2) what is said at meetings with customers will be documented to the extent that the meetings are replaced by email correspondence. The board has decided to set the project in motion, starting in three months and lasting for 12 months, even though Anna Billinger has pointed out that, in her opinion, it is a risky project.

Peter Olsen and Piotr Patek have discussed the digitalization project over lunch with some of the employees in their departments and with Alice Smith. The salespersons especially are very much against the idea. They argue that the customers expect a visit by a real person, and not a computer call, when discussing a possible renovation project. The salespersons also say that customers may not be in possession of the appropriate software to participate in online meetings.

Alice Smith has expressed that she cannot see how anyone can get a proper impression of the tasks and any issues along the way through a small picture on a computer screen. Furthermore, she states that many of the (possible) customers are beyond their first youth. Maybe they don't like being handled by a computer.

The employees with whom Piotr Patek discusses the problem are more positive. A carpenter says that it would be convenient to be able to have a chat with the boss, more or less immediately via a computer or a smartphone, when a problem arises with a customer. Another employee says that more digitalized communication would make it easier to look up what has been agreed with the customer. However, other employees are more reluctant about the project because it would be new to them to use computers for this purpose. They also say that computers are fragile and valuable and can be damaged or stolen. It will therefore be a hassle to work in the suggested way. They are also unsure if digitalization is not just a way to save money.

Some foremen are positive about the idea, as they are tired of spending a lot of time on the road, while other foremen are more reluctant to accept the idea. The bricklayer foreman is even very negative and states that this is a project that has been initiated to make them all impressed by Jan Smith's smart skills.

## Case 2 Closing Hot Fire

Burning Fire is a Norwegian business group specializing in the production of wood-burning stoves. It has subsidiaries in several countries. Hot Fire is a subsidiary situated in Kleinstadt, a German town with about 1,800 inhabitants. The distance to the nearest city, Grossstadt, is about 20 kilometres.

Hot Fire has been producing wood-burning stoves from steel plates for 40 years. Hot Fire was originally a family-owned business but has been a fully owned subsidiary of Burning Fire for ten years. Hot Fire currently has 73 employees, with 65 employed in production, five as administrative staff, and three persons in the management team. Hot Fire is the only subsidiary of Burning Fire in Germany.

The board of directors consists of a representative from Burning Fire (chairman), another representative from Burning Fire, a partner from the law firm that Hot Fire normally uses, and two employees:

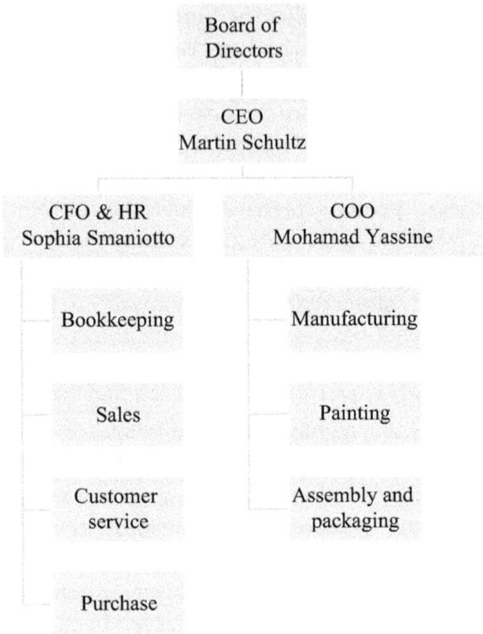


*Figure C.2* Hot Fire organizational chart

one from the administration staff and one blacksmith, who is also a union representative.

The management team consists of CEO Martin Schultz, CFO and HR manager Sophia Smaniotto, and COO Mohamad Yassine, who is both production manager and technical manager. In production, 45 of the employees are semi-skilled workers without any formal training. The remaining 20 workers are trained as blacksmiths. Production is divided into three departments: manufacturing (20 blacksmiths, including a foreman and 20 semi-skilled workers), a painting department (10 semi-skilled workers, including a foreman), and assembly and packaging (15 semi-skilled workers, including a foreman).

In manufacturing, large steel sheets are transformed into thin steel sheets that are cut and shaped into the required shapes and sizes. The production is centred around two large iron press machines of many tons, two cutters, and a bender. Cutters and benders are all very large and heavy. There is little equipment in the painting department and in assembly and packaging. The administration is under CFO and HR manager Sophia Smaniotto. It comprises a bookkeeping clerk, a customer service employee, two salespersons, and one person in procurement.

In the previous year, Hot Fire had an annual turnover of around €13 million. Revenue has fallen steadily from approximately €20 million across the last four years due to a diminishing turnover. This has led Burning Fire to a decision to close the factory and instead produce the stoves at their factory in Poland. The stoves will continue to be sold in Germany under the Hot Fire brand.

Now, at the end of the year, a project to close Hot Fire and move the production to Poland has been established. The plan is that production will be shut down on 1 April next year, and the production facilities will be emptied on 1 May. The entire factory is to be closed on 1 July. Production in Poland with equipment from Hot Fire will be up and running on 1 August. It is necessary that three employees – two blacksmiths and one skilled worker – train workers at the Polish factory on how to operate the machines.

As CEO of Hot Fire, Martin Schultz is responsible for the shutdown. Martin Schultz is most concerned with the company's reputation and a possible damage to the Hot Fire brand. He is therefore focused on how to deal with the local newspaper, which has heard about the closure of the factory and has asked for an interview about the situation. He is also concerned about possible actions by a member of the local municipal council for the Labour Party who lives near the factory.

Martin Schultz has discussed various aspects of the lockdown in the management team. Opinions are divided on how the management should handle the dismissal of employees, which is a consequence of the shutdown of the factory.

CFO and HR manager Sophia Smaniotto is worried about the employees' future. Therefore, she wants to help them find a new job as soon as possible. She says that she has already been contacted by several employees who are worried about their future and their ability to find a new job. She also mentions that Hot Fire will probably be contacted by the local job centre as soon as they hear about the possible layoffs, as they will be worried about unemployment in the municipality.

Mohamad Yassine does not agree with this view. He believes that it is important to keep production running at full scale for as long as possible. He is particularly concerned that the blacksmiths who are necessary for steelwork can find new employment much more easily than the rest of the workers. Mohamad Yassine also mentions that the blacksmiths might be against passing on their knowledge and experience to the Polish workers. After the latest meeting of the board of directors, Mohamad Yassine had a talk with one of the representatives from Burning Fire about a possible career path for himself within the concern. This talk made it clear that his prospects depend on his ability to keep production running until Hot Fire is shut down.

## Case 3 Green transition in Best Brakes

Best Brakes is a company situated in a city of 200,000 inhabitants in a small industrial area next to a bungalow house neighbourhood. The company produces and sells car brakes to car manufacturers. Best Brakes is one among many global producers of brake discs and drums, but it is a leader in Europe on shims, with a market share of 47%. Best Brakes has an annual turnover of around €20 million. The primary results have fluctuated in recent years, with a high in 2017 of €2 million and a low in 2019 of €400,000. Best Brakes was founded in the 1950s as a family business. The company has not been in the family's possession since 2003. Currently, management and an external Polish investor own Best Brakes. The CEO owns 20% of the shares, while the CFO and the COO each own 5% of the shares. Martin Faldowski, the external investor, owns the remaining 70% via his private investment company.

Best Brakes employs 58 people. The management team consists of CEO Leszek Kraskowski, head of finance, administration, sales, and engineering Shiram Venkatraman, and head of operations and procurement Hassan Salim. The board of directors consists of Lilly Holmes, an experienced board member with a background in company law, the management team (who are shareholders), the external investor, and two employee representatives.

Across the year 2021, the management team and the board of directors have discussed possibilities for stabilizing the primary result. In this context, the board has discussed in detail if they need to develop new production methods because customers in the future

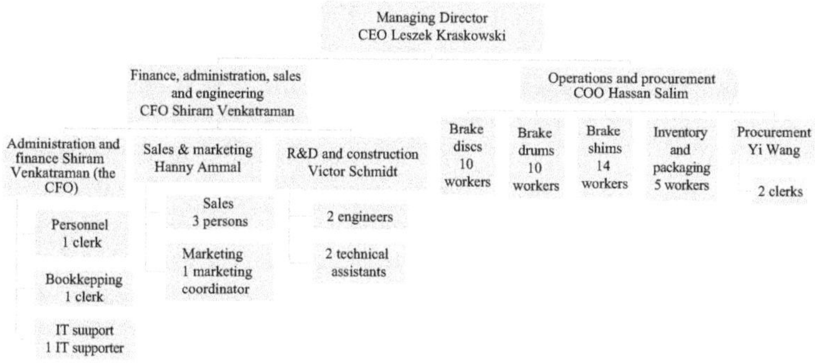


*Figure C.3* Best Brakes organizational chart

may require that production uses sustainable materials and methods. They are also concerned that legislation will soon set up requirements for sustainable production methods. In particular, the COO Hassan Salim is concerned by rumours that the EU will within ten years forbid the type of rubber coating that Best Brakes presently use on the shims. Further, Hassan Salim points out that production leaves quite a large amount of waste rubber. This is problematic, as the only way to get rid of this rubber at present is to burn it, which is problematic for the environment. In addition, the production is quite energy demanding, adding to the $CO_2$ footprint that Best Brakes leaves.

As a result of their discussions, the board has decided to establish a project that will set a green transition of Best Brakes in motion. The project will start on 1 February and run for 12 months. They have communicated this decision to the organization in general terms. The green transition project should result in more sustainable production methods with less waste of rubber, less use of energy, and at least 20% of the energy used produced on site by either windmills or solar panels. Best Brakes has the option to set up solar panels on a nearby field which they own. The company originally bought the field in 1990 to have the possibility of enlarging the production facilities. The field has been grassland as long as anyone can remember. Currently, local citizens use the field to walk dogs, play football, etc.

The COO, Hassan Salim, is very positive towards the advantages of embracing the green transition. However, he points out that such a transition will require a massive investment that will not generate revenue for the first couple of years. Not all employees are equally positive. Hanny Ammal, who is responsible for sales and marketing, points out that the brake market is tough, and that there are several competitors in the market who will try and take over customers if Best Brakes augment their prices. This is especially a threat in the market for shims where Best Brakes up to now could earn a larger margin than in the market for drums and discs where the products are more generic. Hanny Ammal believes that the customers will be unwilling to pay a surplus price for sustainably produced brake parts. This situation may be aggravated if the brakes become less durable with a sustainably produced coating.

## Case 4 Separate sewerage of surface water in the city of Happytown

Happytown is a municipality with a couple of small towns, rural areas, and the main city Happytown with 100,000 inhabitants. Happytown municipality has decided that all roof and surface water must be separated from wastewater by the end of 2032. The municipality is about to plan a project for the needed sewer separations to meet this requirement.

The sewer separation work will be challenging in Happytown city, as the reorganization of the sewer system involves extensive construction work in the city's streets. When implementing separate sewerage, the old pipe in the road, for roof and surface water as well as wastewater, will be renovated using a sock lining, and an additional pipe will be laid down next to it. The old pipe will then be used exclusively for wastewater, and roof and surface water will be led into the new pipe. In some places, the old pipe is very worn. If this is the case, it may be necessary to take the pipe out of operation and instead lay two new sewer pipes – one for roof and surface water and one for wastewater.

Affected landowners, i.e. private landowners, companies, and the municipality, will be ordered to separate the sewer system on their own land. The municipality is a landowner, because parts of the roads are municipal, just as several squares and other areas in the city are owned by the municipality.

Several stakeholders are involved in the sewer separation project. It will be administered by the planning and environmental administration in Happytown municipality. Happytown Supply, an independent limited company that is 100% owned by Happytown municipality, is responsible for carrying out the work. The responsible department within Happytown Supply for carrying out the sewage separation is the Department of Plan & Project, which is part of the Department of Water & Wastewater. Happytown Supply engages many subcontractors to carry out the work, including a major construction company. In addition, they engage an engineering firm as advisor on the sewage separation.

The sewer separation project is complicated by two other projects. The first project is a ten-year plan for replacing the worn sewer network, which is currently five years into the process. The second project is the "Green Castle City" project, initiated by Happytown municipality, with the aim of beautifying the town. This project involves, among other things, the establishment of green areas in the city, especially along the streets in the inner city. The municipality has involved various interest groups with a green agenda in this project.

Persons associated with some of these interest groups have argued that it is in many places possible to avoid changes to the sewer system or at least avoid replacing the old pipes. This is possible if enough green zones are established in the right way in the city, because much less rainwater then needs to be removed by the sewer. Other persons argue that rain gardens along the roads will affect the traffic infrastructure, which is already challenged by narrow roads with bicycle paths. They therefore prefer that roof and surface water be drained away via the sewer network. There is also a debate in Happytown Newspaper and in the Facebook group "Us who live in Happytown" about the financing of the two projects and the sewer separation project. Very prominent debaters, including the chairman of the Happytown Citizens' Association, point out that some landowners may have to pay for other landowners to have a green oasis, because some of the cost of establishing and maintaining the green areas may be moved from the project "The Green Castle City" to the sewer separation project. The debate also includes representatives from the local business community, who expect lost revenue, perhaps in several rounds, because the same roads are dug up several times in connection with several, independent projects and maintenance works.

## Case 5 Exercise at work

Carl Hansson is HR director at Fun Play, a company that develops and produces toys. The company has 2,500 employees. Fun Play has salaried employees (50%) and hourly paid employees (50%). The hourly paid employees are employed in production and packaging, while the salaried employees are employed in the development department, in various management functions, and in the administration.

Carl Hansson is much concerned with ensuring that employees thrive, so that they can perform at their best, and at the same time be happy and satisfied with their workplace. He has just been at a very inspiring event, where the speaker talked about the importance of physical exercise. The company has up to now made several half-hearted attempts at encouraging the employees to exercise, including furnishing a room with fitness equipment, which unfortunately is only utilized very little.

Carl Hansson wants to encourage the employees to exercise as part of their daily routines. The company can do so by paying for membership in a fitness club or by participation in sports events. However, Carl Hansson finds that a much better solution is to give employees the opportunity to exercise at Fun Play during working hours, as this would enable more employees to exercise than if it took place in the employees' spare time.

It is fairly easy to implement an initiative that allows the salaried employees to exercise during working hours, because they can manage their own time. The company already has a gym, and the employees can go to the gym for an hour during the workday, if they can fit this into their work schedule. However, this will probably not happen because of the company culture. Several employees have expressed that they would feel like they were shirking work if they went to the gym during working hours instead of doing work tasks. They said that they expect their colleagues to feel the same way, and therefore they would think badly of them if they did go. They are therefore not prepared to do so, and they also expect the same of their colleagues.

As for the hourly paid employees, it is difficult to see how it is possible to let them use the company's gym during working hours. These employees typically work on an assembly line that they can only leave during set breaks. If an employee leaves the assembly line to go to the gym, the tasks for which this employee is responsible will not be done, and production therefore will stop. This will have consequences for the business's ability to deliver goods to customers on time. However, there is always buffer staff ready at the assembly line, so it is possible to free up employees for half an hour during their working day, if no one is on sick leave, i.e. if all seats on the assembly line are occupied.

Carl Hansson wonders a lot about whether all employees should be offered the same – and what it should be. Or whether it is perhaps better to offer alternative options. To learn more about what will happen and try different solutions before asking the management for resources to roll out new initiatives to the entire company, he will carry out a pilot project that will develop initiatives that will be tested in two departments before they are rolled out to the entire company.

Carl Hansson has decided that the pilot project will take place in two departments that differ in important aspects. He does not worry about funding for the project as Fun Play is very well consolidated.

One department is a salaried department, namely Fun Play's IT Service Centre. There are 50 employees here: 15 software specialists who deliver software to the entire company, 15 hardware specialists who prepare and deliver computers, and 20 employees in the company's IT service desk. The service desk is open 24 hours a day, with employees working in three shifts. The employees at the service desk take turns being on the different shifts. The other two areas are only open during the day. Among the 50 employees, there is a manager for each of the three areas.

The other department is production. There are 350 employees here, of whom 240 are hourly paid and work in three shifts around the clock on an assembly line. The shifts are fixed, i.e. the same employees workday, evening, and night shifts. There are six day teams, two evening teams, two night teams, and two weekend daytime teams. Night and weekend shifts are cancelled in July and August. During these months, all workers work on different shifts to make up for vacation vacancies. There are 14 middle managers employed for the 12 teams (so there is always a buffer of two in order for there to be room for courses, holidays, illnesses, etc.).

Among the hourly paid workers in production, there are three union representatives. Carl Hansson is worried how they will react to the pilot project. At previous occasions, Carl Hansson had clashes with them, e.g. about changing the food in the canteen. The union representatives find that the company has no right to interfere with the employees' way of life. They are against the pilot project because they are afraid that there will be an A-team and a B-team, where the A-team consists of slim, well-trained people, who eat healthily and exercise with pleasure, while the employees on the B-team will become more and more stigmatized as someone who cannot live up to the company's expectations. They also suspect that top management only thinks about the bottom line, and that cost saving is the real purpose of the project, which is just disguised as employee well-being and benefits.

## Case 6 Preparing Magnificent Tea Tree Oil for export

Magnificent Tea Tree Oil is a company that produces and markets a range of products for skin care and personal hygiene based on tea tree oil. Magnificent Tea Tree Oil employs 39 people, including the managing directors.

The company exclusively sells its own-produced "Magnificent Tea Tree Oil" brand. Magnificent Tea Tree Oil is a market leader in Denmark for this type of product. Up until now, Magnificent Tea Tree Oil has distributed its products in Denmark through health-oriented retailers with physical stores and online shops as well as online-only retailers. In addition, Magnificent Tea Tree Oil sells its products through its company web shop.

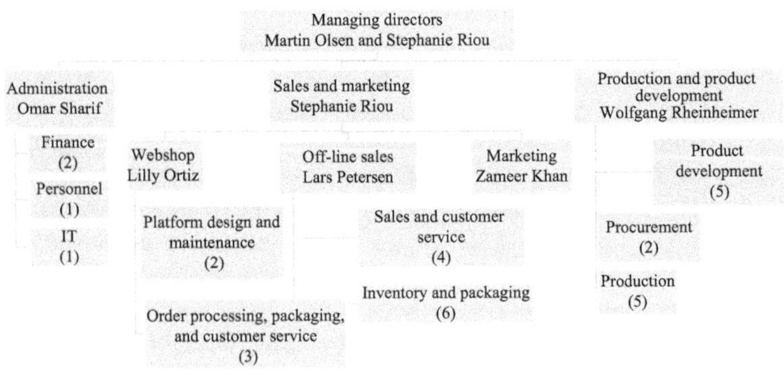


*Figure C.4* Magnificent Tea Tree Oil organizational chart

The information on the packaging is in English, German, and Danish. This has allowed some import by health-oriented shops in Germany. The sales made by these importers accounted for 5% of the turnover in 2022. Magnificent Tea Tree Oil has, during the last two years, had an annual turnover of approximately €3.5 million, and the company has operated with an annual surplus before tax of around €530,000.

The company started in 1990 as a family business and has since then had various owner constellations. Since 2015, the company has been owned by a capital fund together with a varying number of managing directors. At present, there are two managing directors, Martin Olsen and Stephanie Riou. They each own 20% of the shares.

The owners have a shared ambition for the company to grow based on the company's own production, under the Magnificent Tea Tree Oil brand. They are determined to keep the brand identity that they have built over the years. The owners feel that the Danish market is saturated, limiting their opportunities to grow through market penetration, and they have therefore looked for other options and decided to engage in export to various markets within the EU. As a starting point on this adventure, the owners have decided to establish a project that will facilitate a market launch in Germany and Austria. This project will act as a pilot project for export to additional countries.

The managing directors expect that the pilot export project will result in additional demand corresponding to ten times the present production. They therefore contemplate how to accommodate this demand. As a part of this, they discuss whether their present suppliers will be able to meet the demand. They are worried about their main supplier of chemical additives being able to accommodate the additional demand. The managing directors therefore consider completely replacing this supplier. The managing directors also discuss how much they will need to adapt their marketing strategy to the new countries, and how to handle social media internationally, as they have no experience in this matter. Furthermore, the managing directors discuss how it might be a challenge for their present sales force and customer service employees who are only used to working in Danish (and in English to a limited extent). The managing directors wonder in particular whether the customer service employees are equipped to communicate with German-speaking customers.

# Appendices

# Appendix A: Assessing the stakeholder's intention to contribute

| *Stakeholder* | *Expected consequences of contributing* | *Influences from social norm and perception of fairness* | *Perceived ability to do the act* | *Intention to contribute* |
|---|---|---|---|---|
| | | | | |
| | | | | |
| | | | | |

Note: This is an empty version of Table 5.2.

# Appendix B: The stakeholder register

| *Stake-holder* | *Possible influ-ence* | *Necessary contribu-tions* | *Require-ments and wishes* | *Inten-tion to con-tribute* | *Challenges and opportu-nities* | *Category and need for attention* |
|---|---|---|---|---|---|---|
| | | | | | | |
| | | | | | | |
| | | | | | | |

Notes: Dark grey=high need for attention, light grey=some need for attention, white=no need for attention now

1 Stakeholder. Who are the individuals or entities that can influence or be influenced by the project? Write either role or name (or both).
2 Possible influence. How and to what extent can the stakeholder influence or be influenced by the project, and is it positive or negative? (Table 4.1)
3 Necessary contributions. How does the project need the stakeholder to contribute? What should the stakeholder do or not do? (Table 4.2)
4 Requirements and wishes. What does the stakeholder require or want to contribute?
5 Intention to contribute. Is the stakeholder positive or negative towards contributing as necessary or desired? Use the elements behind the intention to contribute to assess this. (Table 5.2)

6 Challenges and opportunities. Are the stakeholder's requirements urgent and/or legitimate? What can strengthen the intention to contribute? How can an intention to contribute be put under pressure or supported? Can the stakeholder form networks with other stakeholders? (Figure 4.2)

7 Category and need for attention. Choose from the categories in Table 6.1 and use different shades of grey to mark the need for attention.

# Appendix C: The action plan

| *Stake-holder with category* | *Chal-lenges and opportu-nities* | *Stra-tegy* | *Engag-ement tactics* | *Plan-ned actions* | *Com-muni-cation* | *When* | *Respo-nsible* |
|---|---|---|---|---|---|---|---|
| | | | | | | | |
| | | | | | | | |
| | | | | | | | |

Notes: Dark grey=high need for attention, light grey=some need for attention, white=no need for attention now

1. Copy stakeholders with category and challenges and opportunities from the stakeholder register (Table 6.2). Challenges and opportunities can be supplemented by additional information on communication challenges.
2. Decide strategy, engagement tactics, and actions (Table 8.2) based on (1).
3. Decide communication based on decisions in (2). Use Figures 9.1 and 9.2, Tables 9.1–9.3, and Boxes 9.1 and 9.2.
4. Plan when the actions will take place. Use the time considerations (Box 9.3).
5. Who is responsible for each stakeholder? This person is responsible for following up on planned activities. We recommend that each stakeholder has one contact person in the project organization, so that the stakeholder always knows who to turn to if there are any questions.

# Index

Tables are referred to in bold.

For Product Safety Concerns and Information please contact our EU representative GPSR@taylorandfrancis.com
Taylor & Francis Verlag GmbH, Kaufingerstraße 24, 80331 München, Germany

www.ingramcontent.com/pod-product-compliance
Ingram Content Group UK Ltd.
Pitfield, Milton Keynes, MK11 3LW, UK
UKHW022344190926
475702UK00015B/2086
*9781041169031*